Contents

Key:

Core concepts
Research concepts
Introduction to Sociological theories

Agency and structure

Central to Sociology is the debate about how far individuals behave according to their free choice and how far their behaviour is due to the influence of the society surrounding them. Rather than agency *versus* structure, agency *and* structure seems more appropriate as they influence each other; the individual has an impact on the society and the society has an impact on the individual.

Agency

Agency is the idea that individuals are 'agents' in society; they can exercise power and influence over it. They are not victims pressurised by social forces beyond their control (Layder, 2000). Instead, they have free will and as a result are able to make choices. The structure of society is still important, but it is seen as rising out of the actions of individuals. For this reason, agency is sometimes referred to as **action** and the individuals as actors.

Agency is based on a **micro theory** of society; this is the small-scale study of human behaviour which looks at the day-to-day experiences and feelings of people.

Structure

While individuals clearly make choices in society, the structure of society has a strong influence on them. Most of Sociology emphasises structure over agency; the society over the individual. Those who advocate the importance of structure do not focus on how actors interpret their roles, but instead on how people's roles are influenced and shaped by the society. Individuals are constrained by the society they live in; for example, being in poverty will have a huge impact on the individual regardless of the meaning they attach to it, and they are likely to struggle as an individual to change this situation. Structure is based on a **macro theory** of society; this is the large-scale study of

human behaviour in society as a whole. It examines the roles of institutions in society such as education, the family and the legal system and how these affect people's lives beyond their control.
In summary:

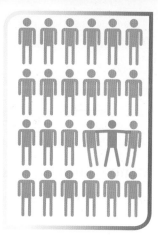

Agency	Structure
Individual	Society
Micro theory	Macro theory
Choice	Constraint
Free will	Social control
Independence	Socialisation

Key theories

Two theories that emphasise agency	Key names	Key ideas
Weberianism	Weber Ritzer Rex and Tomlinson (neo-Weberians)	It is important to interpret the meanings of the actions that individuals take. These are referred to as **social actions**. To find the meaning of an action, we need to discover the reason or motive for the action taking place.
Symbolic interactionism	Mead Blumer	This addresses interpersonal action – how people deal with each other and the shared meanings of symbols that help us understand society; e.g. a handshake is a symbol of a greeting and a mark of respect. Individuals understand the symbol because of the shared meaning attached to it.

Two theories that emphasise structure	Key names	Key ideas
Functionalism	Durkheim Parsons Davis and Moore Merton	This theory is based on consensus. Society is held together in social solidarity because people generally reach an agreement on what is important; there is a value consensus. Society operates like the human body – different institutions work together for the good of the whole.

Two theories that emphasise structure	Key names	Key ideas
Marxism	Marx Engels Gramsci Althusser	Society is based on a conflict between the proletariat or working class (the exploited majority) and the bourgeoisie or ruling class (the powerful minority). It is held together by power, authority and force.

Structuration (structure + action)

Anthony Giddens (cited in Haralambos & Holborn, 2000) attempted to reconcile the dualism of agency and structure with his theory of structuration. Giddens argued that structure and agency (action) go hand in hand; one could not exist without the other. It is social action which creates structures that are reproduced and evolve over time. Society has been achieved by action, but action has been constrained or shaped by the structure.

Consider yourself reading this book. This may be a result of agency based on your individual choice to read it now instead of watching TV, but it can also be placed in the context of structure; you may have been told to read the book by your teacher.

Think about ...

Are there any aspects of life over which the individual has total control?

See also: Nature versus nurture; Socialisation; Sociological imagination.

References

HARALAMBOS, M. & HOLBORN, M. (2000) *Sociology: Themes and Perspectives*. 5th Ed. London: HarperCollins Publishers.

LAYDER, D. (2000) *Understanding Social Theory*. London: Sage Publications.

Anomie

Anomie means 'normlessness' or a lack of the norms which maintain order and stability in society. A state of anomie exists when the rules and laws regulating the behaviour of the individual in society have weakened. The moral fibre of society becomes disrupted, making crime and deviance more likely.

Durkheim and anomie

For Emile Durkheim, organic solidarity was vital for society to operate effectively. It is the social cohesion or glue that bonds individuals together because of their dependency on each other in their working relationships. They rely on each other for the goods and services they need. At times (such as the move from simple to advanced societies), the rate of change in the economy outpaces the moral regulation of society and anomie occurs. However, Durkheim argued that once people had adapted to advanced society, anomie would cease to be a problem. (Durkheim, 1893)

According to Durkheim, anomie is one of the causes of suicide in society. A lack of regulation upsets the balance of people's lives, for example in times of economic boom and bust, or following a divorce or a redundancy.

Merton (cited in Fulcher & Scott, 1999) stated that for some people the pressure to be successful in society caused them to deviate against norms in order to achieve their goals. This was particularly true when the structure of society limited their chances of success, for example a lack of educational qualifications or living in poverty during a recession. Such individuals might turn to crime as an alternative way to achieve success. In a society where the end goal such as 'to get rich quick' is more important than the means, such as hard work, people's conformity to the norms of society weakens.

In August 2011, the riots that took place in UK cities such as London, Manchester and Birmingham, when people looted shops in their own communities, could be seen as an example of anomie. In these cities there is a paradox as huge amounts of consumer goods are available, often being marketed as things people need rather than want. However, the products on sale are not affordable to many of the residents, particularly in a recession.

For Merton there are four responses to anomie. They are applied here to the goal of becoming wealthy:

1. **Innovation:** The individual rejects law and turns to crime to achieve the goal, for example committing fraud or being a gang member.

2. **Ritualism:** The individual decides there is no chance of becoming wealthy and rejects the goal. They continue to work, but without attempting to secure a pay rise or promotion. They see their lives as beyond their control.

3. **Retreatism:** Both the means and the ends are rejected. The individual has in some ways dropped out of society; they may be unemployed or homeless.

4. **Rebellion:** Both the means and the ends are rejected, and are replaced by alternatives. Such individuals may choose to live alternative lifestyles, perhaps based on self-sufficiency, rejecting capitalist values.

Think about ...

Explain how anomie would cause problems in the education system. (Think of the school rules as norms.)

See also:
Functionalism;
Norms; Organic
analogy.

References

DURKHEIM, E. (1997) *The Division of Labor in Society*. Introduction by COSER, L. A. New York: Free Press.

FULCHER, J. & SCOTT, J. (1999) *Sociology*. Oxford: Oxford University Press.

Assimilation

Assimilation is the process in which an immigrant group completely adopts the way of life of their new country. They take on the norms and values of the country they have moved to and abandon those from their country of origin.

Mass immigration to the UK

From the 1950s to the 1970s during a period of mass immigration from the Caribbean and South Asian countries, the UK government believed assimilation was the best policy. The belief was that if immigrants behaved in the same way as the natives, there would be less conflict over cultural differences. However, it is difficult for people to lose their old way of life, and many would argue it is undesirable. The diversity of the UK makes it culturally rich and interesting. Assimilation was abandoned as an impractical and unethical policy to be replaced by multiculturalism. This involved different ethnic groups living side by side, following the norms and values of their country of origin and also British culture.

Bussing

'Bussing' is when children from different ethnic minority groups are 'bussed' to schools outside their local area. It was practised in the UK in the 1960s in a controversial policy to assimilate recent immigrants. In 1965, the Department for Education and Science produced a document recommending that immigrant children should make up no more than a third of the total population of a school or class. The document was titled 'Spreading the Children', implying that Local Education Authorities should share the 'burden'. Very few LEAs adopted the policy; in those that did, children had to travel far from home and were vulnerable to bullying. The policy was made illegal in 1975. It was considered racist as no white children were bussed.

Citizenship test

Those wishing to become a British citizen must pass a test called Life in the UK. This could be seen as an example of assimilation as the test includes questions about the national anthem, battles in British history, and English literature, as well as practical issues of everyday life. However, it could be argued that the test is to help people integrate into British culture without having to abandon their own ethnic identities.

Reverse assimilation

An expectation that recent arrivals will assimilate into British culture is perhaps difficult when it is hard to define what is meant by 'British culture'. While some groups have assimilated more than others, what has also happened is that some white British people have adopted the cultures of the groups of people who have moved to the UK. This is called 'reverse assimilation' and applies particularly to young people growing up in multicultural cities. They are influenced by a wide range of ethnic groups' fashions and music which have become an integral part of youth culture. Rather than trying to copy other ethnic groups, for many it is more a case of sharing the same cultural identity regardless of differences in skin colour.

Think about ...

Do you think citizenship tests are important? Answer the questions on the Life in the UK website (see References).

See also:
Hybridity;
Multiculturalism.

References

HOME OFFICE UK BORDER AGENCY Life in the UK Test. [Online] Available from: http://lifeintheuktest.ukba.homeoffice.gov.uk. [Accessed: 13th February 2013].

TOMLINSON, S. (2008) *Race and Education: Politics and Policy in Britain*. Maidenhead: McGraw-Hill Education. Open University Press.

Beanpole family

In 2003, Julia Brannen identified a growing number of 'beanpole' families. These are multigenerational families with few members in each generation. They are caused by a greater life expectancy and people having fewer children than in the past. The structure is long and thin, hence the term 'beanpole'.

Example of a beanpole family

Traditional family: Jack was born in 1912. He had three sisters and two brothers. His parents were married. He had five uncles, five aunts and 20 cousins, but no surviving grandparents.

Beanpole family: Jack was born in 2012. He has no siblings and is raised by his single mother. Jack has one aunt, one uncle and two cousins. His grandparents still work full-time and his great-grandmother is almost 90.

Beanpole families sprout social change

Beanpole families – those with fewer children and multiple generations of older people – are leading to profound social changes, government statisticians warned yesterday. The beanpole effect was the outcome of a nationwide 'pruning of the family tree', the Office for National Statistics said. Fewer brothers and sisters in one generation leads to fewer aunts and uncles in the next. So, instead of a 'bushy' family tree with lots of branches, there are longer, thinner patterns of family relationships. More great-grandparents are surviving into their eighties and nineties, and there are fewer young siblings.

"We are in the midst of one of the most striking demographic shifts for generations, as the ageing of the population becomes a reality," said Penny Babb, editor of the 2003 *Social Trends*, published yesterday. "The number of people aged 65 and over

> in the UK has increased by more than half over the past 40 years...it is projected to exceed the number of young people under 16 in just 11 years' time."
>
> (Carvel, 2003)

The sandwich generation

This concept was coined by Dorothy Miller (1981) to describe adults who are involved in the care of their ageing parents, while also supporting their own children.

For many people in their 50s and 60s in the UK today, the idea of 'winding down' to retirement and relaxing is far removed from the reality. Instead, this generation is often 'sandwiched' between looking after ageing parents, financially supporting their adult children (who may be unemployed or struggling to pay off university debts) and caring for their grandchildren. With the removal of a compulsory state retirement age and the need to support themselves financially for years to come, they are likely to be still working full-time, in addition to spending time caring for others.

Think about ...

Identify the two main causes of the rise in beanpole families.

See also: Cereal packet family.

References

BRANNEN, J. (2003) Towards a Typology of Intergenerational Relations: Continuities and Change in Families. *Sociological Research Online*. 8 (2).

CARVEL, J. (2003) Beanpole Families Sprout Social Change. *The Guardian*. 30th January. [Online] Available from: http://www.guardian.co.uk/society/2003/jan/30/britishidentityandsociety.uknews. [Accessed: 3rd January 2013].

MILLER, D. (1981) The Sandwich Generation: Adult Children of the Ageing. *Social Work*. 26. p.419–423.

Canteen culture

'Canteen culture' can be defined as 'a set of conservative and discriminatory attitudes said to exist within the police force' (Oxford English Dictionary). Lower-ranking officers, who tend to be white and male, regularly work long hours together and as such have a strong sense of group solidarity which develops into their own 'canteen culture'.

The police bond of identity

Research has shown that members of the police force are relatively isolated from wider society and often feel as though they are under public scrutiny. This bond of identity can make it difficult for individual officers to become separate from the group, and often questionable attitudes and practices are hidden from outsiders. As a result, any research done will not always yield **valid** results. (Webb et al, 2009)

Background: ethnicity and criminal justice

Statistics show that, in the UK, ethnic minorities are more likely to be stopped and searched by the police. Black people are seven times more likely and Asians twice as likely to be stopped. In the year 2006–2007, Asians were three times more likely to be searched than the white majority under the Terrorism Act 2000. One way of explaining the ethnic differences at each stage of the criminal justice system is as a result of racism.

Coretta Phillips and Benjamin Bowling (2007) found that many officers held negative stereotypes of ethnic minorities and this led to deliberate targeting for stop and search by the police. It is believed by sociologists that negative stereotypes are reinforced by the canteen culture among lower-ranking officers. (Haralambos & Holborn, 2000)

Why does 'canteen culture' develop?

Jerome Skolnick (1966, cited in Moore et al, 2009) claimed that officers categorise and stereotype people because of the training they have received on how to spot potential troublemakers. Statistics support the fact that those they 'spot' are often young, male and regularly from ethnic minorities, therefore racial stereotyping occurs. He also believes that due to the police upholding the values of the state, conservative values prevail. When traditional conservative values are applied to a group mainly of white working-class males, with a strong sense of solidarity and a degree of social isolation, it is easy to see how a 'canteen culture' of prejudiced attitudes thrives.

Think about ...

What can be done to prevent a 'canteen culture' from developing within the police?

See also:
Institutional racism.

References

HARALAMBOS, M. & HOLBORN, M. (2000) *Sociology: Themes and Perspectives*. 5th Ed. London: HarperCollins Publishers.

MOORE, S., AIKEN, D. & CHAPMAN, S. (2009) *Sociology A2 for AQA*. London: Collins Educational.

WEBB, R., WESTERGAARD, H., TROBE, K. & STEEL, L. (2009) *A2 Sociology*. Brentwood: Napier Press.

Capital

Pierre Bourdieu used the term 'capital' to refer to economic, cultural and social assets that enhance an individual's life chances and therefore have the power to increase social mobility. Bourdieu (1977) identified three forms of interconnected capital: economic, cultural and social.

Economic capital

An individual has great economic capital if they have a large income from their occupation or substantial wealth from their assets. These assets might include stocks and shares, land and property. The passing down of wealth through the family maintains an elite wealthy minority in society. Income and wealth are very unevenly distributed in the UK. The richest 10 per cent are more than 100 times as wealthy as the poorest 10 per cent. (Hills et al, 2010)

Cultural capital

This involves knowledge and appreciation of high culture and a high level of education. Bourdieu (1984) used the term 'cultural capital' to explain differing levels of educational attainment by social class. He argued that middle-class parents transmit cultural capital to their children which helps them in school; for example, the books read at home, the newspapers bought and the visits to museums give middle-class children an advantage in school because they have prior knowledge and understanding.

Social capital

This refers to the increased **life chances** an individual gains due to their social connections with others. For example, a boy attends a prestigious public (fee-paying) school because his father studied there. He gains a high level of cultural capital from his education and wins a place at an elite university. On completing his degree, he begins work in a successful company owned by a family friend who happens to be an 'old boy' of the same school. His social connections give him **status** within the company and he becomes very wealthy. This is sometimes known as an 'old boys' network'. In this case, it's not what you know but who you know that matters.

Examples from research

The Up series

In this documentary we see how differing levels of economic, cultural and social capital affect an individual's life chances. It is a longitudinal study directed by Michael Apted which revisits a group of people from very different backgrounds every seven years.

The documentary began in 1964 when the participants were seven years old. Three of the participants, John, Charles and Andrew, attended a prestigious public school that gave them great access to cultural capital; for example, in one scene the viewer sees the boys at seven years old singing 'Waltzing Matilda' in Latin and discussing their favourite broadsheet newspapers. John demonstrates significant social capital by attending public schools and then studying at Oxford University. He became a barrister and also gained social capital through his marriage to the daughter of an ambassador to Bulgaria (Bruzzi, 1997).

The Benefits of Facebook 'Friends'

In this 2007 study of Michigan State University students, Ellison et al found that students maintained their social capital by keeping in touch with school friends from their hometowns on Facebook. Today, many people use social networking for creating and maintaining friendships, for finding new relationships and for business opportunities. For Ellison et al, it therefore serves as a powerful form of social capital.

Think about ...

1. Is who you know more important than what you know today?

2. Does having a thousand friends on Facebook make an individual more socially connected or socially isolated?

See also: Habitus; Life chances; Social class; Status.

References

BOURDIEU, P. (1984) *Distinction: A Social Critique of the Judgement of Taste*. London: Routledge.

BOURDIEU, P. (1977) *Outline of a Theory of Practice*. Cambridge: Cambridge University Press.

BRUZZI, S. (1997) *Seven Up!* London: British Film Institute.

ELLISON, N. B., STEINFIELD, C. & LAMPE, C. (2007) The Benefits of Facebook 'Friends': Social Capital and College Students' Use of Online Social Network Sites. *Journal of Computer-Mediated Communication*. 12 (4). Article 1. [Online] Available from: http://jcmc.indiana.edu/vol12/issue4/ellison.html. [Accessed: 14th September 2012].

HILLS, J. et al (2010) *An Anatomy of Economic Inequality in the UK – Summary: Report of the National Equality Panel*. London: Centre for Analysis of Social Exclusion. London School of Economics and Political Science.

Cereal packet family

The traditional nuclear family has been described as the 'cereal packet family'. This is the popular image of the family often promoted in adverts for 'family-sized' packets of breakfast cereals, cars and a range of other consumer goods. According to Edmund Leach, this family type is seen as the norm because it is commonly portrayed as such by the media.

Characteristics of a cereal packet family

The cereal packet family consists of a man and woman who had children after they were married. The parents have never been married before and have traditional roles of male as breadwinner and female as housewife.

The media often reinforce the dominant ideology of the traditional nuclear family. In reality, there is no such thing as a typical family in Britain and less than 5 per cent of the population live in a traditional nuclear family with a male breadwinner and a housewife caring for two children. (OECD, 2011)

Contemporary UK families

In reality, families and households in the UK today are far removed from the cereal packet image as the following trends show:

Families and households today	Evidence (England and Wales)
1. There are more households without children than with them.	In 2008, approximately 65% of households had no children. (OECD, 2011)
2. Many women are childfree.	Over 20% of women born in 1965 have not had children. (OECD, 2011)

Families and households today	Evidence (England and Wales)
3. The majority of mothers are in paid employment.	In 2007, approximately 60% of mothers of dependent children were in paid employment. (OECD, 2011)
4. There has been a rise in the number of children born outside of marriage.	In 1980, approximately 10% of births were outside of marriage compared to around 40% in 2007. (OECD, 2011)
5. Many children are raised by single parents.	Single parents with dependent children represented 26% of all families with dependent children in 2011. (ONS, 2011)
6. Many gay couples live together.	In 2011, there were 105,000 people in civil partnerships. (ONS, 2012)

New Right commentators might perceive the above trends as negative for society. The cereal packet family image retains its appeal perhaps for nostalgic reasons of looking back to the so-called happy family images of 1950s Britain. However, there have always been problems in families. Postmodernists welcome the diversity of family life as a reflection of increased choice in society and growing tolerance.

Think about ...

Can you identify any adverts that reflect the diversity of family life?

See also:
Conjugal roles;
Warm bath theory.

References

OECD (2011) *Doing Better for Families*. [Online] Available from: http://www.oecd.org/els/familiesandchildren/47701118.pdf. [Accessed: 4th February 2013].

ONS (2012) *Families*. Office for National Statistics. [Online] Available from: http://www.ons.gov.uk/ons/taxonomy/index.html?nscl=Families. [Accessed: 4th February 2013].

Confluent love

Confluent love can be defined as being a love which is subject to change. It is very different from **romantic love**, which has a sense of 'forever' and a 'one and only' ideal.

Many sociologists have observed that changes in the structure and nature of the family have taken place over time.

Changes in the nature of family

The traditional image of the nuclear family (a family unit of mother, father and children) is associated with the 1950s, when this structure was commonplace and based on romantic love and monogamy. In today's society, things are changing. Although the nuclear family remains dominant, there is a huge diversity in family structure, with rising divorce rates, an increase in lone-parent families and the legalisation of civil partnerships all contributing to this change.

Giddens and love

In his work *The Transformation of Intimacy* (1992), Anthony Giddens claims that romantic love has been replaced with confluent love in today's society. As society becomes increasingly individualistic, fluid and diverse, the structure of intimate relationships is also changing. Giddens describes the advent of 'plastic sexuality', which in turn promotes the new confluent love ideal.

For Giddens (1992), plastic sexuality refers to a new freedom in sexual expression; sex is no longer tied up with reproduction and marital relationships. In the postmodern era, we have a more developed sense of 'self', and with this comes a liberty to choose with whom and when to have a sexual relationship, rather than valuing virginity highly as was the case in the past.

This 'plastic sexuality' translates into a confluent love-based 'pure relationship', which, according to Giddens, is the new relationship ideal, based on negotiation, equality and ultimately the choice to remain part of the relationship. Today, people choose whether or not their relationships continue, and only remain in them if they are beneficial to both partners. A feature of such relationships is what Giddens refers to as a 'rolling contract', which means that each partner knows that at any point the relationship could be terminated by the other equal partner. (Noll, 2005)

Perhaps Giddens' theory is more of an ideal than a reality for many people, but he claims that this is the way we are moving, and this development clearly parallels the emergence of postmodernity. If people are looking for a 'pure relationship' based on confluent love, rather than a traditional form of relationship based on romantic love, this may explain the rise in divorce rates and variety of family forms that are present in today's society.

Think about ...

Read a news article debating same sex marriage. Then explain why Giddens believes confluent love and the pure relationship are replacing romantic love in today's society.

See also:
Conjugal love.

References

GIDDENS, A. (1992) *The Transformation of Intimacy: Sexuality, Love and Eroticism in Modern Societies*. Cambridge: Polity Press.

HARALAMBOS, M. & HOLBORN, M. (2000) *Sociology: Themes and Perspectives*. 5th Ed. London: HarperCollins Publishers.

NOLL, S. (2005) Three observations on love, marriage and the future of Anglicanism. [Online] Available from: http://www.virtueonline.org/portal/modules/news/article.php?storyid=2567. [Accessed 4th February 2013].

Conjugal roles

Conjugal roles are the roles of husband and wife, or of partners in a relationship, in the home. The splitting of tasks such as cooking, cleaning and organising the family finances is called the domestic division of labour. In some homes, this is shared equally and interchangeably; in other homes, roles are segregated. Despite some moves towards equality, studies show that women still do the majority of housework and childcare even when they work full-time in paid employment.

'The Good Wife's Guide'

In the 1950s, the magazine *Housekeeping Monthly* published 'The Good Wife's Guide', which gave a list of instructions to women on how to keep their husbands happy. These included:

➤ having dinner ready when he gets home from work

➤ touching up make-up and hair before he arrives

➤ keeping the children quiet

➤ listening to his problems even if the wife has some of her own

➤ knowing her place.

Of course, the advice may not have been strictly followed, but nevertheless it was a clear sign of patriarchy (male dominance) in the home. During the 1950s, few women worked full-time in paid employment. By the 1970s, more women had entered the workforce and some researchers believed that conjugal roles became more equal.

The symmetrical family

In the 1970s, Michael Young and Peter Willmott argued that the family was becoming more symmetrical because of a 'march of progress' in which family roles were evolving to gradually become more equal. They researched the conjugal roles of married couples in London in the early 1970s and stated that there was no work in the home that was strictly reserved for wives. From their survey they found that 72 per cent of a sample of 1,928 married men working full-time reported that they had helped their wives at least once a week with household tasks other than washing up. (Young & Willmott, 1973)

Ann Oakley claimed, however, that while this percentage might initially seem impressive, it becomes less so when we consider that if men did only one task in an entire week such as ironing their own clothes, they would be included in this 72 per cent. Oakley therefore dismissed the idea that this was convincing evidence of symmetry. (Oakley, 1985)

Wife work

'Men get one thing from marriage that women never do… wives.' (Maushart, 2002)

According to Susan Maushart, at the turn of the twenty-first century marriage remained a very unequal partnership which benefited men at the expense of women. She points to the fact that the majority of divorces are requested by women as evidence of women's dissatisfaction with marriage. Maushart cited research by Heidi Hartmann that a husband creates eight hours of extra work per week for his wife. She also claimed that women do more emotional care-giving in a relationship, such as offering comfort to their partner following a difficult day at work (Maushart, 2002). This is similar to Jean Duncombe and Dennis Marsden's view that women work a triple shift: housework, paid employment and emotional work (Duncombe & Marsden, 1995). Maushart claims that even sex is part of wife work; while most women enjoy sex, it is still a way in which women service the needs of their partners at the expense of their own.

Equality in the homes of same sex couples

With improved rights including civil partnerships and a proposal for same sex marriage (approved in 2013), more gay and lesbian couples are living together in formally recognised relationships. Jeffrey Weeks claims that same sex relationships are based more on equality than heterosexual relationships. This is logical as same sex couples do not have a tradition to follow and therefore are less likely to fall into stereotypical roles. However, in reality anyone can have a lazy partner who does not pull their weight around the home, gay or straight!

Problems of researching conjugal roles

A key problem of researching conjugal roles is that most studies are based on time use surveys, or they ask a couple how much housework they do. There are validity problems with this approach. The data gathered may not be accurate because the individual might forget what they did and when, or they might overestimate the amount of housework they did to avoid appearing lazy.

One way of overcoming this problem is to base research on observations. This was the approach adopted for the BBC programme *Who Does What?* (2011) in which couples gave permission to be filmed in their homes. The couples were individually asked to guess what percentage of a certain task they did in the week, such as cooking, cleaning and ironing. There was a considerable difference in the guesses of both partners and the reality of who did what. However, this method also has flaws as people tend to change their behaviour when they know they are being watched.

Moving towards more equal roles

A key way to change who does what in the home in the UK is to change parental leave arrangements, which are among the most unequal in Europe. In 2013, women can take up to 12 months' maternity leave (some of which would be unpaid) compared to men having only two weeks' leave as an entitlement by law. It is therefore not surprising that many couples fall into traditional conjugal roles.

In Spain, a more radical step has been taken to address inequality and 'machismo'. Spanish marriage contracts contain a requirement for men to share housework with their wives. The new law has led to the invention of a washing machine called 'Your Turn' that uses fingerprint recognition so that the same person cannot do a load of washing twice in a row, and an iron that has heavy weights hanging down, giving men a workout while doing the ironing! (BBC News, 2005)

Think about ...

What is the division of labour in your family or household? Who does what? Is there gender equality?

See also: Cereal packet family.

References

BBC NEWS (2005) Housework looms for Spanish men. [Online] Available from: http://news.bbc.co.uk/1/hi/world/europe/4100140.stm. [Accessed: 15th February 2013].

BBC2 (2011) Who Does What? [Online] Available from: http://www.bbc.co.uk/programmes/b00xxgx7. [Accessed: 15th February 2013].

DUNCOMBE, J. & MARSDEN, D. (1995) Workaholics and Whingeing women: Theorising Intimacy. *Sociological Review*. 43.

MAUSHART, S. (2002) *Wifework: What marriage really means for women*. London: Bloomsbury Publishing.

OAKLEY, A. (1985) *The Sociology of Housework*. Oxford: Basil Blackwell.

RETRO HOUSEWIFE (2006) The Good Wife's Guide. *Housekeeping Monthly*. 13th May 1955. [Online] Available from: http://www.retro-housewife.com/good-wife-guidelines.html. [Accessed: 15th February 2013].

YOUNG, M. & WILLMOTT, P. (1973) *The Symmetrical Family: A Study of Work and Leisure in the London Region*. London: Routledge.

WEEKS, J., HEAPHY, B., and DONOVAN, C (1999) *Partners by choice: Equality, power and commitment in non heterosexual relationships*. In Allan, G. (ed.) *The sociology of the family: A reader*. Oxford: Blackwell.

Consumer culture

Consumerism is the belief that buying more and more goods and services confers advantages on the individual and society. In a consumer society, individuals base their identity not on how they earn their money, but on how they spend it. The slogan used by Selfridges during a sale encapsulates this: 'I shop, therefore I am', which is a play on the words of the philosopher Descartes, 'I think, therefore I am'.

The power of consumerism

In a consumer society the individual buys a product not only for its functionality, but for the message it gives about their status; for example, wearing a Rolex watch denotes wealth. Everything from the make of car they drive to the supermarket they use might say something to others about the identity of the consumer. However, the ability to spend depends on social class and therefore it can be argued that consumerism has not replaced occupational status as a source of identity; rather, the two go hand in hand.

Consumer as king

'The consumer has become a god-like figure before whom markets and politicians alike bow.' (Gabriel & Lang, 1995)

The apparent rise in consumer choice, consumer demand and laws to protect consumer rights seems to suggest consumer power. In a time of recession, the individual demands value for money, forcing retailers to cut their margins. In recent years, there has been a growing popularity of programmes such as *Watchdog* focusing on consumer rights.

It could be assumed that Coca-Cola represents the great power of the massive transnational company which produces it. However, in the 1980s, the consumers' reaction to the company's plan to change the flavour of the drink is an excellent example of consumer power. Consumers felt that the drink belonged to them and that the company could not change the flavour as they pleased. The company had to revert to the original flavour. (Pendergast, 1993, cited in Mackay, 1997)

Consumer as victim

The consumer can be disempowered by debt and poverty and in this case becomes pawn rather than king. The existence of credit lenders leads to poorer people in society becoming vulnerable to debt with many paying high rates of interest, not on luxuries but on household essentials such as gas and electricity because they are being bought on credit. The consumer can also fall victim to illegal money lenders (loan sharks), or to savings schemes such as Christmas savings clubs which may go bust so that the consumer loses their money.

Consumer as criminal

The advertising of goods to those who cannot afford them was seen as one of the reasons for the August riots of 2011 in the UK, during which many people looted shops in city centres across the country. The consumer crime of shoplifting disadvantages consumers in general through the incorporation of shoplifting costs into store prices.

Anti-consumerism

Some people try to reject the influence of consumerism in their lives. They may do this by being self-sufficient, for example by growing their own vegetables. They may also choose to shop at independent shops rather than giving more money to transnational companies. They may boycott certain companies because they disagree with their values; for example, if a story is in the media about the use of sweatshops or testing on animals, consumers may choose to switch companies. However, this is replacing one form of consumerism with another.

According to Tim Edwards, the best way an individual can become empowered is to reduce their consuming: 'this choice to switch off their televisions, close their magazines and think about something else is the most practised form of consumer opposition, and is the truest measure of resistance in consumer society'. (Edwards, 2000)

Think about ...

1. Give examples of popular consumer goods and what their ownership signifies.

2. Identify examples of ways in which the consumer can exercise power in today's society.

See also:
Culture;
Globalisation.

References

EDWARDS, T. (2000) *Contradictions of Consumption: Concepts, Practices and Politics in Consumer Society*. Buckingham: Open University Press.

GABRIEL, Y. & LANG, T. (1995) *The Unmanageable Consumer: Contemporary Consumption and its Fragmentation*. London: Sage Publications.

MACKAY, H. (ed.) (1997) *Consumption and Everyday Life*. London: Sage Publications in association with Open University Press.

Correspondence principle

The correspondence principle (sometimes known as 'correspondence theory') is a concept used by neo-Marxists Samuel Bowles and Herbert Gintis to describe the relationship between education and the workplace. They identify a correspondence between the authority relationships governing interaction in school and the stratified relationships found in the workplace.

Bowles and Gintis

For Bowles and Gintis, it is the needs of the capitalist economy rather than the needs of the students which shape the education system (Bowles & Gintis, 1976). They argue that schools in a capitalist system reproduce rather than reduce inequalities in society. They claim that schools integrate young people into the economic system in the following ways:

➤ **Teaching students to accept authority:** Hierarchies exist in the school which correspond to the hierarchies in the workplace. Students are expected to follow the rules of the school and later in life they will have to follow the rules given to them by their employers in order to keep their jobs.

➤ **Promoting the norms and values required in the workplace:** Students in schools often receive certificates for excellent attendance. Poor attendance will result in disciplinary action, as would occur in the workplace.

➤ **Teaching students about the importance of self-presentation and conformity:** Students might be given a detention for wearing trainers or sent home if they wear a nose stud or are considered to be wearing too much make-up.

➤ **Encouraging students to be motivated by external rewards:** These include academic qualifications which correspond to the reward of pay in the workplace. According to Bowles and Gintis, in both school and the workplace people derive little enjoyment from the work itself; therefore external rewards are needed to motivate them to work harder.

➤ **Teaching students that inequality is fair:** If other students do better in a test, it is because they are cleverer or worked much harder; while in many cases this might be true, students are not told that their results differ also because of their different class backgrounds (at least not until they study Sociology!). This corresponds to the workplace where employees are encouraged to see the pay rise of a senior colleague as fair on the basis of their hard work.

Bowles and Gintis were critical of the American school system. They hoped instead for:

➤ an egalitarian system (based on equality) that attempts to overcome inequalities rather than widen them, and for school to compensate for the inequalities in the wider society

➤ education to be developmental, giving students the freedom to be creative individuals who do not feel pressure to conform to the demands of a capitalist society.

Criticisms of the principle

Bowles and Gintis wrote their book in the 1970s. Today there is more of a focus on equal opportunities in schools and the wider society. Critics claim that:

➤ students are rewarded for creativity and independent thought (consider the introduction of A level Critical Thinking)

➤ listening to the student voice has been a focus of
school inspections

➤ not all teachers are agents of capitalism. (In the 2010s,
many teachers participated in strike action over their
pensions and cuts to public services, and in doing so
they arguably demonstrated their dislike of aspects of
capitalism.)

Far from there being a strong link between education and
the workplace, Nick Barham found in his 2003 study that
there was a feeling among the young people he spoke to
that school had little to do with preparing them for the
world. They questioned the relevance of what they were
learning. (Barham, 2006)

Think about ...

How far do you think that what you have learned so far
in your education has corresponded to the workplace?
(Consider both the formal learning and the hidden
curriculum.)

See also: Hidden
curriculum;
Marxism;
Meritocracy.

References

BARHAM, N. (2006) *Disconnected*. London: Random House.

BOWLES, S. & GINTIS, H. (1976) *Schooling in Capitalist America*. London:
Routledge.

COLE, M. (1998) *Bowles and Gintis Revisited*. London: Routledge and
Kegan Paul.

Culture

Culture, in the sociological sense, means the way of life of people in a society, including the languages they speak, the food they eat, the clothing they wear, the television programmes they watch, schooling, and sports and music. Everyone has culture, but the way culture is expressed varies between societies and between groups within the same society. Culture is taught to the individual through the process of socialisation. It is therefore learned rather than natural.

Characteristics of culture

One of the earliest sociological definitions of culture was given by Edward Tylor and is still applicable today: 'Culture is that complex whole which includes knowledge, belief, art, morals, law, custom, and any other capabilities and habits acquired by man as a member of society' (Tylor, 1903). We can simplify this by stating that culture comprises norms, values and symbols:

➤ **Norms** – rules or guidelines that define what is seen as appropriate behaviour in society. Traditional British norms include queuing, eating roast dinner on Sundays, drinking tea, and playing cricket, football and rugby.

➤ **Values** – general shared principles about human behaviour in society. Traditional British values include freedom of speech, democracy and having a 'stiff upper lip' (not expressing signs of emotional difficulty).

➤ **Symbols** – objects used to represent something else. Symbols are used to convey meaning: for example, to some the British Bulldog represents Winston Churchill's character during the Second World War. Other traditional British symbols include Big Ben, red telephone boxes, the Royal Family, and fish and chips.

Why is culture essential for society?

Culture is what links the individual to the wider society. The Jamaican activist Marcus Garvey argued that:

'A people without the knowledge of their past history, origin and culture is like a tree without roots'. In order to be a member of society, the individual needs to have been socialised into its culture. The vital importance of culture to society is evident when we examine the rare cases of children who have missed out on primary socialisation due to severe neglect and abandonment. Such children are commonly referred to as 'feral' (meaning wild).

High culture and popular culture

When a person is described as 'cultured', this means they have an appreciation of high culture. Examples of high culture are classical music, opera, ballet and classic literature, such as the works of Chaucer.

Popular culture, by contrast, has much wider appeal. Examples include chart music and soap operas. However, the line between the two forms of culture is subjective. For example, Shakespeare's plays might be considered high culture as they are literary classics and the language is considered inaccessible by some; however, all school children in the UK learn about Shakespeare, and within his lifetime Shakespeare's plays had a wide appeal to the working class.

Sociologists are generally not interested in rating one form of culture as more or less valuable than any other. Everyone has norms and values and therefore sociologists are more likely to consider everyone in society to be cultured.

Think about ...

What would feature on your list of British norms, values and symbols? Does Britain have a distinct culture?

Reference

TYLOR, E. (1903) *Primitive Culture: Researches into the Development of Mythology, Philosophy, Religion, Language, Art, and Custom*. London: John Murray.

See also:
Multiculturalism;
Nature versus
nurture; Norms;
Socialisation;
Subculture;
Values.

'Dark side' of family life

The 'dark side' of family life refers to violence within the family, including domestic violence and child abuse. The existence of a 'dark side' to family life provides a sharp contrast to the functionalists' harmonious 'warm bath theory'. The 'dark side' of family applies to all types of families and also cuts across social class, age, ethnicity and sexuality.

Domestic violence

‘Domestic violence is the abuse of one partner within an intimate or family relationship. It is the repeated, random and habitual use of intimidation to control a partner. The abuse can be physical, emotional, psychological, financial or sexual.’ (Refuge, 2010)

Here are some key statistics on domestic violence:

➤ Two women are killed every week in England and Wales by a current or former partner. (Homicide Statistics, 1998)

➤ Approximately one in four women experience domestic violence in their lifetime. (Council of Europe, 2002)

Common myths about domestic violence

Myth	Reality
More women would leave if the abuse was bad.	There are many reasons why women stay: fear for their lives and their children's safety, financial dependency, a belief that their partner will change, love, worn down self-esteem, etc.
An abuser has just lost their temper or is out of control.	Systematic abuse is a reflection of maintaining power and control, not losing it. Abusers can be selective about when they hit their partner, e.g. when the children are asleep. Many abuse their partners emotionally, without anger or physical violence. This shows the extent of their control.
Men do not suffer from domestic violence.	The ManKind Initiative reports that approximately one in six men experience domestic abuse in their lifetime. There is a problem of underreporting; men are three times less likely to report abuse to the police than women are.

(Refuge, 2010, and the ManKind Initiative, 2012)

How can domestic violence be explained?

Feminists introduced the issue of domestic violence into the study of families and households. They explained violence against women as an extreme form of male power over women. Although the issue of domestic violence and abuse is mostly discussed in terms of male on female, both men and women can be victims.

Russell and Rebecca Dobash carried out research at a refuge for women in Scotland. In their study, *Violence Against Wives* (1979) they explained wife assault in relation to the cultural expectations about male authority in marriage. Women in the study said that violence tended to happen when they had not responded to husbands' immediate needs or when they had questioned men's actions and opinions. Arguments between husbands and wives commonly ended when the husband decided it should, and if the wife persisted, violence would result. Dobash and Dobash found that women from all social classes were affected and that violence was not the action of disturbed individuals, but of men who were regarded as 'normal' in the wider society. However, patriarchy cannot explain male victims of female abusers. It could be argued that men are victims of domestic violence for the same reasons as women.

Child abuse

Child abuse is the term used when an adult harms a child or young person under the age of 18. It can take four forms, all of which can cause long-term damage to a child: **physical abuse**, **emotional abuse**, **neglect** and **sexual abuse**. There is often a link between **domestic violence** and child abuse. Here are some key statistics:

➤ Every ten days in England and Wales, a child is killed at the hands of their parent. In almost two thirds (65 per cent on average) of cases of children killed at the hands of **another** person, the parent is the principal suspect.

➤ In the vast majority of cases, children know their abusers. In April 2010, abuse by strangers constituted only 5 per cent of all abuse cases in the UK. (NSPCC, 2012)

How can child abuse be explained?

Sociological explanations of child abuse often focus on poverty; for example, that poverty creates a sense of frustration which leads to aggression. However, the apparent link between child abuse and poverty may be due to the tendency to see working-class families as more prone to abuse than middle-class families. Child abuse in lower-income families is more likely to be spotted due to the increased contact such families have with local authority officials, such as social workers. Like domestic violence, child abuse happens in all types of families.

Statistics reflect the concerns and priorities of government and local authorities. For example, in the 1950s, little was known about the sexual abuse of children, but by the mid-1980s registrations for sexual abuse rose dramatically. Statistics possibly say more about changes in child protection concerns than they do about the extent of child abuse.

What is defined as child abuse varies from culture to culture and over time. For example, since 2005, smacking a child and leaving a mark has been illegal. (It is not, however, illegal for a parent to smack their child otherwise.) Some people consider smacking children to be a form of child abuse whereas others do not.

Media scaremongering and moral panics?

A moral panic results following widespread public concern that an event or group is threatening society. There has been a moral panic in the early years of the twenty-first century regarding child safety and paedophilia. Children are often warned of 'stranger danger' but child abuse is often committed by someone known to the child, such as a parent or other relative. It could be argued that children are not significantly at a greater risk today than they were 50 years ago, but the risk is **perceived** to be greater due to sensational media coverage.

Think about ...

Domestic violence is a significant killer of young women in the UK. Why does it seem to get less attention in the media than other causes of death?

See also: Moral panic; Warm bath theory.

References

DOBASH, R. & DOBASH, R. (1979) *Violence Against Wives: A Case Against the Patriarchy*. New York: Free Press.

MANKIND INITIATIVE (2012) *Male victims of domestic violence and partner abuse: 21 key facts*. [Online] Available from: http://www.mankind.org.uk/pdfs/21KeyFacts_Jul2012. [Accessed: 23rd December 2012].

NSPCC (2012) *Child Homicide Statistics*. [Online] Available from: http://www.nspcc.org.uk/inform/research/statistics/child_homicide_statistics_wda48747.html. [Accessed: 23rd December 2012].

REFUGE (2010) *Domestic Violence – The Facts*. [Online] Available from: http://refuge.org.uk/get-help-now/what-is-domestic-violence/domestic-violence-the-facts. [Accessed: 23rd December 2012].

Deskilling

Deskilling refers to the reduction of skilled labour in an industry in order to save time and money. This usually occurs due to the rise of automation: the use of machinery and technology in place of people in order to increase productivity and cut down staffing costs.

What is deskilling?

Writing from a Marxist perspective, Harry Braverman (1974) claimed that the workplace was characterised by deskilling. Consider an individual who works on a factory assembly line; rather than using a range of skills they repeat the same task over and over again. Braverman stated that the worker therefore experiences boredom in their job and feels alienated (or detached) from their work because they do not get the satisfaction of seeing the product from design to completion.

Deskilling is a means by which the bourgeoisie can exploit the proletariat by justifying lower pay for fewer skills.

Examples of deskilling

➤ Cashiers in shops using automatic tills instead of having to work out the correct change themselves.

➤ Drivers of black cabs in London have to pass a demanding exam called 'The Knowledge' which requires knowledge of over 25,000 streets. However, many private hire taxis now use satellite navigation systems instead of relying on this skill.

➤ Some teachers fear that their profession is being deskilled by the employment of unqualified teachers. In 2013, about 10 per cent of teachers in free schools (outside local authority control but funded by the state) did not have formal teaching qualifications. (Boffrey, 2013)

Deskilling or 'upskilling'?

It could be argued that rather than deskilling, many occupations have undergone a process of 'upskilling'. Although Braverman claims that computers have taken away skills, the learning of new skills is required to use them. Many people in society today have experienced redundancy and have had to learn new skills in order to gain employment.

Think about ...

'Computers have deskilled employees and students.' How far do you agree with this statement?

See also: Fordism; Marxism.

References

BOFFREY, D. (2013) Free school head without any teaching qualifications plans to ignore curriculum. *The Observer.* 10th March. [Online] Available from: http://www.guardian.co.uk/education/2013/mar/10/free-school-head-no-qualification. [Accessed: 10th March 2013].

BRAVERMAN, H. (1974) *Labor and Monopoly Capital: The Degradation of Work in the Twentieth Century.* New York: Monthly Review Press.

Deviance

Deviance means going against expected norms of behaviour. While most crimes are seen as deviant (such as stealing from a shop), many acts of deviance are not crimes (for example, swearing in class). Deviance is a social construction; in order to define behaviour as deviant it has to be judged from the perspective of the norms of a social group or community.

Behaviour that is labelled as deviant varies by culture.

Deviance is dependent on context

As the examples below illustrate, what is considered deviant in one culture may be an accepted social norm in another:

➤ Eating with the hands: in the UK it is considered correct etiquette to use a knife and fork when eating a meal at the table with others. Eating with the hands at a formal meal would be deviant to this norm. In India, however, eating with the hands is the norm.

➤ Cannabis: although widely used as a recreational drug in the UK, cannabis is illegal and its usage is still seen as deviant by many. In 2009, the drug was reclassified from class C to class B. However, in Amsterdam, the use of cannabis is generally tolerated and can be purchased in small quantities from 'coffee shops'.

From deviance to an accepted norm

Behaviour that was once considered to be deviant may be seen as an accepted norm over time. Until 1967, homosexuality was not only considered deviant, but also criminal in the UK. Today, gay people have gained rights and acceptance in society. Since 2005, gay couples have had the option to enter into a civil partnership, giving them equal rights to married heterosexual couples, such as pension and inheritance rights. The Equality Act 2010 makes it illegal to discriminate on the grounds of sexuality.

From an accepted norm to deviance

Behaviour that was once an accepted norm may come to be seen as deviant over time. In the past, the link between smoking and cancer was unknown; in fact, in the 1920s, some doctors even recommended smoking as being good for nerves. It was also seen as a sign of sophistication. It was not until fairly recent times that smoking has been seen in a negative light. The link between smoking and cancer is now medically undisputed and a smoking ban has been in force in England since 2007. Arguably, smokers have gone from the fashionable to the excluded in society.

Primary and secondary deviance

Primary deviance

This was defined by Lemert (1967) as behaviour which goes against societal norms, but is tolerated by members of society. It is seen as exceptional behaviour in an otherwise norm-abiding person. For example, a student does not do their homework because of problems at home, or an individual shouts at a friend in the 'heat of the moment' but later apologises.

Secondary deviance

This is when the behaviour is not excused but instead is stigmatised. The individual is labelled as deviant by society and may therefore engage in further deviant behaviour. The deviance therefore becomes amplified. For example, if a student is excluded from school they might feel rejected by the institution and engage in anti-social behaviour.

Think about ...

Make a list of activities that would be seen as deviant in the family but acceptable social norms in a peer group.

See also: Moral panic; Social control.

Reference

LEMERT, E. (1967) *Human Deviance, Social Problems and Social Control.* Englewood Cliffs, NJ: Prentice-Hall.

Disneyization

Disneyization is a concept coined by Alan Bryman to describe the ways in which society increasingly displays features of the Disney theme parks. Bryman (2004) identified four features of Disneyization.

Features of Disneyization

1   Theming
This is when a theme is applied to an organisation, though that theme may have little to do with the organisation's function. It gives a common identity.

➤ Alton Towers – like Disney World, the amusement park now includes a water park and a themed hotel. Visitors can stay in different themed rooms including the Peter Rabbit Room and the Arabian Nights Room. Most amusement parks are now called theme parks.

➤ The Trafford Centre – a shopping centre and leisure complex in Greater Manchester with an extravagant theme. It features a food court called the Orient which is in the style of a steamship. The food court is spilt into different 'worlds' including China, Morocco and Italy.

2   Hybrid consumption
This is when different forms of consumption are combined to generate more profit. Shopping, entertainment and dining become one experience without differentiation. It is no coincidence that in many amusement parks and museums the visitor has to walk through the gift shop to leave the premises. For example, Alton Towers has shops, restaurants, a water park, hotels and a golf course.

3   Merchandising
Here are two examples:

➤ In some television shows for children, it is the toy, not the programme, which is made first and as a result the television show becomes an advert for the toy.

➤ University students can buy goods such as hoodies emblazoned with the university name and motto from a shop on the campus. These give the wearer a common identity, but also advertise the university.

4 Performative labour

This refers to retail workers and those in the hospitality industry being expected by employers to put on a show or performance and behave like actors. Bryman also referred to this work as emotional labour. It involves acting because rather than displaying what they might be feeling, such as boredom or tiredness, staff exhibit constant happiness. For example, they will often end a transaction by wishing the customer a nice day. Employees are taught that the customer is always right and to treat them as such.

Performative labour relates to the work of Erving Goffman who stated that individuals were actors who put on performances in their working lives. The shop floor or restaurant is the front region or stage where the workers adopt the identity required by the company. The shop stockroom and the restaurant's kitchen are back regions where the workers can briefly drop the persona away from the audience, the customers. (Goffman,1971)

Think about ...

Look for examples of Disneyization in your nearest town or city. Consider themed restaurants and shopping centres.

See also:
Consumer culture; Fordism; McDonaldization.

References

BRYMAN, A. (2004) *The Disneyization of Society*. London: Sage Publications.

GOFFMAN, E. (1971) *The Presentation of Self in Everyday Life*. Harmondsworth: Penguin Books.

Empty-shell marriage

The concept 'empty-shell marriage' refers to an arrangement whereby a couple remain living together and legally married, but the relationship as it once was is now over and they lead separate lives.

Definition of empty-shell marriage

William Goode states that empty-shell marriages are similar to marriages that end in divorce:

'Most families that divorce pass through a state – sometimes after the divorce – in which husband and wife no longer feel bound to each other, and look on one another as almost a stranger. The "empty-shell" family is in such a state. Its members no longer feel any strong commitment to many of the mutual role obligations, but for various reasons the husband and wife do not separate or divorce.' (Goode, 1993)

Reasons for empty-shell marriage

Despite the relative ease of obtaining a divorce following the 1969 Divorce Reform Act, a couple might remain in an unsatisfactory marriage for a number of reasons:

➤ **Staying together for the sake of the children:** Some couples are unhappy, but believe that it will be better for their children, and easier to share childcare, if they remain living together.

➤ **Religion:** Despite increasing secularisation, a divorce may be harder to obtain in some religious communities.

➤ **Social standing:** A couple stay living together to 'keep up appearances'. This might be particularly relevant for individuals with high profile occupations under the attention of the media who wish to protect their status, for example politicians.

➤ **Routine and apathy:** A couple's relationship is not working, but they have fallen into a routine. The marriage is unsatisfactory, yet in some ways comfortable and they fear the loneliness of separation.

With the removal of stigma regarding separation and divorce, together with the growing economic independence of women, it is difficult to imagine large numbers of empty-shell marriages today. However, the economic recession from 2008 onwards might have caused a rise in numbers. With a fall in house prices, many couples who wish to separate are faced with the stark choice of staying together in the hope that the housing market will improve, or selling their home at a loss.

There are no records of the number of empty-shell marriages. It is very difficult to estimate numbers as such couples may appear to the outside world to be happily married. In addition, they are likely to be listed as married in Census data. The unhappiness some people experience with marriage is concealed in an empty-shell marriage. This particularly applies to countries where a divorce is difficult to obtain because of religion.

Think about ...

Identify arguments for and against staying together 'for the sake of the children'.

See also: Cereal packet family.

Reference

GOODE, W. (1993) *World Changes in Divorce Patterns*. Yale: Yale University Press.

Ethics in research

The term 'ethics' derives from the Greek *ethikos* (meaning character), and is interpreted as a way of deciding actions which can be called 'good' or 'moral'. In sociological research, this is an important consideration, especially in a study of a controversial or sensitive nature. A sociologist undertaking research must always consider the impact on the participant, both during and after the research process.

Ethical practice in research

The British Sociological Association (2002) has a set of professional guidelines for ethical practice which include a code of conduct relating to responsibilities towards subjects, covert research (when people do not know they are being researched), integrity and relationships with subjects. These guidelines are voluntary, but to get approval and funding for a project, the researcher may have to submit proposals to an ethics committee. This would be a particular concern if the study involved children, prisoners, other vulnerable people, or health issues. (Harvey et al, 2000)

Key issues that must be considered

1   Possible harm
The subjects of research must not come to any physical or psychological harm. In 1961, Albert Bandura (cited in McLeod, 2011) conducted a study to investigate whether aggressive behaviours could be acquired by children imitating what they saw. He conducted an experiment involving 72 children, aged from three to six. The children were divided into groups, with some exposed to an adult behaving violently towards a toy called a 'Bobo doll'. The children who watched the aggressive behaviour tended to respond in a more violent way towards the doll themselves. For Bandura, these results supported his Social Learning Theory that behaviour could be learned through imitating another person.

In terms of ethics, this study raises questions about the possible harm the children could have come to, either through observing the violent behaviour during the experiment or the lasting impact on them after the research.

2   Informed consent

The participants should give their informed consent to being part of the research. 'Informed consent' implies that the subjects are aware of the purposes of the research and have agreed to participate in it.

However, the researcher must be careful as being too open about their study could, in some cases, compromise the results. This is known as the Hawthorne effect and it occurs when a subject knows they are being studied and then behaves or responds differently as a result. This observer effect would impact upon the validity of the results gained.

Some sociologists therefore opt for covert research methods which mean that the subjects are not aware they are participating in research. Covert research raises several other ethical issues:

➤ This method involves deception.

➤ The safety of the researcher could be compromised.

➤ If relationships are built up with subjects, they could be very hurt or withdraw from the study when they find out.

3   Confidentiality and privacy

Protecting the confidentiality and privacy of research subjects is a vital ethical consideration. Depending on the nature of the study, the findings could have a major impact on the subjects once they are published, or could compromise their personal and professional lives.

In a study in the 1960s, Laud Humphreys was criticised for risking the personal and professional lives of men he studied. Humphreys engaged in research to investigate factors which lead to the culture in America of some men, often married and middle-class professionals, using public toilets for casual homosexual activity. Following this participant observation, Humphreys then went covertly to the homes of some of the men and conducted door-to-door surveys to gain further information about their family and professional status. From an ethics point of view, this study raises many concerns, particularly in the area of privacy and confidentiality. The university department in which Humphreys was a researcher also felt that the research was unethical.

Think about ...

You have been commissioned by the local authority to conduct some research into teenage drug use in the area. Decide which method(s) you think would be most appropriate to use and why. Identify the ethical issues raised by this research.

See also:
Reliability;
Validity.

References

BRITISH SOCIOLOGICAL ASSOCIATION http://www.britsoc.co.uk.

HARVEY, L., MACDONALD, M. & HILL, J. (2000) *Theories and Methods*. London: Hodder and Stoughton.

MCLEOD, S. A. (2011) Bobo Doll Experiment. [Online] Available from: http://www.simplypsychology.org/bobo-doll.html.

STOW COLLEGE (1970) Laud Humphreys and the Tearoom Sex Study. [Online] Available from: http://socialscience.stow.ac.uk/resmethods/research_issuesmats/laud_humphreys.htm.

Ethnocentrism

Ethnocentrism is the focus on one culture with the belief that it is superior to others or at least universal (that it means the same everywhere and the same to everyone). To be ethnocentric is to judge other cultures by the norms and values of one's own culture.

Examples of ethnocentrism

Cousin marriage

Although legal across Europe, cousin marriage can carry a social stigma in Western society. Yet more than 50 per cent of British Pakistanis marry a cousin and approximately 10 per cent of all marriages worldwide are between first and second cousins. (Bittles, 1994)

Arranged marriage

For some, the idea of marrying someone that they have only recently met (or never met) seems unusual. This is because it is difficult not to make judgements based on one's own culture and experiences. In the UK today, most people live together before marriage. In an arranged marriage, the focus is on love *after* marriage. It is worth noting that for many young South Asians in the UK there is a trend towards 'love' marriage where the couple are already in a relationship and the marriage is negotiated between both partners and their families with more flexibility than may have been the case in the past.

Day of the Dead

In Mexico, the lives of loved ones who have passed away are celebrated every year with a week of festivities beginning with a national holiday called *Día de los Muertos* (Day of the Dead). Sugar skulls are given as gifts to both the living and the dead. Towns are decorated with skeletons and skulls. Death is celebrated. This is very different from the UK where some consider that morbid.

Ethnocentric curriculum

In Máirtín Mac an Ghaill's study *Young, Gifted and Black*, a group of girls called the 'Black Sisters' were critical of the school's curriculum because of the focus on imperialism and British colonialism. They felt that black history was ignored. Here it could be argued that the curriculum was ethnocentric, favouring the history of the white British middle classes. However, note that Mac an Ghaill's study was in the late 1980s and since this time there has been a greater effort to reflect the diversity of students' ethnic backgrounds in what is taught; for example, many schools celebrate Black History Month.

Cultural relativism

To avoid ethnocentrism, it is considered good practice in Sociology for researchers to follow the concept of cultural relativism. This means that the researcher should try to understand the culture from the viewpoint of the group being studied, and to view behaviour in the context of the way of life of the group. Despite opinion to the contrary, it does not mean that sociologists have to be accepting of everything. Researchers will have their own standards, but should try to see their own norms and values as specific to their culture and not as a point of reference for measuring the experiences of others.

Think about ...

Can you think of any British traditions or customs that might seem unusual to people elsewhere in the world?

See also:
Assimilation;
Culture;
Verstehen.

References

BITTLES, A. H. (1994) The role and significance of consanguinity as a demographic variable. *Population and Development Review*. 20. p.561–584.

MAC AN GHAILL, M. (1988) *Young, Gifted and Black: Student–Teacher Relations in the Schooling of Black Youth*. Milton Keynes: Open University Press.

Femininities

Femininity refers to the characteristics associated with women. Of course, women are not a homogenous group (they are not all the same). Some people would argue therefore that it is perhaps more accurate to write about 'femininities' rather than 'femininity'.

What is femininity?

In Sociology, femininity is viewed as a social construction. Simone de Beauvoir claimed: 'One is not born, but rather one becomes, a woman.' (de Beauvoir, 1949)

How femininity is defined depends on the culture of society, and the expected roles of women change over time. Traditionally, a feminine identity might include passivity, caring for children and a preoccupation with appearance.

It is a misconception that feminine identities are natural. For example, some people think women are 'naturally better at ironing'. Sociologists would argue that there is nothing natural about ironing, but that women have been socialised into this role. Ann Oakley argued that children are socialised into gendered identities by their parents. One way is by canalisation. This involves channelling a child's interests into toys seen as appropriate for their sex; for example, girls might be given toy kitchens to socialise them into the roles of housewife and mother. This message continues later in life as adverts for cleaning products and baby care tend to be marketed at women.

Appearance

Feminine identities are often associated with appearance. In *The Beauty Myth*, Naomi Wolf claimed that after decades of the influence of feminism, women in developed countries ought to be enjoying more freedom than ever before. However, Wolf argues that women do not feel free and this is due to concerns about physical appearance:

'More women have more money and power and scope and legal recognition than we have ever had before; but in terms of how we feel about ourselves physically, we may actually be worse off than our' unliberated grandmothers. (Wolf, 1991)

Judith Halberstam stated that adolescent girls who display masculine traits are often punished. This can include bullying from the peer group. The pressure on girls to look a certain way could arguably be growing today because of the internet. Girls are able to scrutinise the photos of other girls on Facebook, and make-up videos on YouTube get hundreds of thousands of views. (Halberstam, 1998)

Resistance

Sue Lees discussed the contradictory messages that girls face: they are expected to work hard at school, but being academic risks being seen as unfeminine; they are supposed to be independent, yet do more housework than their brothers; they are told to care about their appearance, but not to look too sexually attractive. In addition, there seems to be a double standard in which young men can have many sexual partners and gain respect from the peer group, whereas young women who do the same risk being labelled 'slags'. Lees does state, however, that girls have become more confident in challenging stereotypes about femininity. (Lees, 1993)

Femininity and cultural difference

Heidi Mirza states that discussions of femininity often ignore cultural differences, assuming a universal experience of womanhood. Mirza argues that far from being universal, ideas about femininity among Caribbean women were different from those of their white peers: Caribbean women did not see differences between women's and men's roles, and there was a desire to be independent from men. (Mirza, 1992)

Think about ...

Girls have outperformed boys in school for over 20 years. Why is appearance perceived as a more feminine characteristic than academic success?

See also:
Glass ceiling;
Masculinities.

References

DE BEAUVOIR, S. (1972) *The Second Sex*. Harmondsworth: Penguin.

HALBERSTAM, J. (1998) *Female Masculinity*. Durham: Duke University Press.

LEES, S. (1993) *Sugar and Spice*. London: Penguin.

MIRZA, H. (1992) *Young, Female and Black*. London: Routledge.

OAKLEY, A. (1972) *Sex, Gender and Society*. London: Temple Smith.

WOLF, N. (1991) *The Beauty Myth*. London: Vintage.

Feminism

Feminism is a theory and social movement which aims to improve the rights of women. It has achieved significant changes but gender inequality still exists. The idea that feminists are man-haters is a myth; most do not hold extreme views, as shown by this quote from Rebecca West: 'Feminism is the radical notion that women are people.' There are different types of feminism but feminists are united in their concern for the welfare of women.

Liberal feminism

This type of feminism is about establishing equal rights between men and women, and has focused on laws. Liberal feminism is associated with the 'first wave' of feminism at the turn of the twentieth century. Prior to this, Mary Wollstonecraft was a pioneering early feminist who wrote *A Vindication for the Rights of Women* (1792), in which she argued that women were treated like second-class citizens; for example, she objected to the use of the word 'man' when referring to people in general.

A major achievement of liberal feminists was gaining the vote for women. These women were called suffragettes. The campaign was led by Emmeline Pankhurst. Women have voted on equal terms with men since 1928.

However, liberal feminists have been accused of neglecting the needs of working-class women and not going far enough in the fight for gender equality. The private sphere of the home and family were also neglected. However, liberal feminism has had a lasting influence on society and its legislation.

Key liberal feminists: Mary Wollstonecraft, John Stuart Mill, Naomi Wolf

Radical feminism

There was a resurgence of feminism in the 1960s (the 'second wave'). Women gained confidence from other social movements of the 1960s and feminism was reformed. A slogan from the second wave of feminism is very relevant to the study of radical feminism – 'the personal is political' meant that every part of women's personal lives could be affected by politics. They therefore looked at how society shaped marriage and motherhood for men's advantage. The main goal for radical feminists is not to introduce equal rights (they do not want women to be like men); instead they want women to be free from **patriarchy** (male dominance).

Some, but not all, radical feminists advocated separatism – a policy that women should cut themselves off sexually and socially from men. For example, Shulamith Firestone (1970) stated that regardless of changes in laws, women would still be at a disadvantage due to childbearing. Firestone advocated the use of contraception, and also reproductive technology (test-tube fertilisation and artificial wombs) to free women from their biology and dependence on men. While separatism can be criticised for being impractical and a policy that most women would not want in practice, it is important not to dismiss radical feminists as being too extreme. They made important contributions to feminism by focusing on topics that had not been addressed before, such as pornography, rape and domestic violence.

Key radical feminists: Shulamith Firestone, Kate Millett, Andrea Dworkin

Marxist feminism

Marxist feminists agree that women are oppressed by men in the family; however, they argue that this is a result of living in a capitalist economy. Wives' unpaid domestic labour is seen as vital for the economy; they look after the current and future generation of workers at little cost to the capitalist.

Sheila Rowbotham (1989) recognised that housework was in fact 'work'. She argued that cleaning and childcare were often not seen as a job and pointed out that if women were paid for this work, they would earn hundreds of pounds every month.

According to Irene Bruegel (1979), women provide a reserve army of labour; they are seen as a cheap source of employment who can be brought into the paid labour force when needed, and then retreat into the family again when they are no longer required. This happened to many women during the Second World War.

In the twenty-first century when most women are in paid employment, Marxist feminist views may seem less relevant. However, women still do the majority of housework and experience inequality in the workplace.

Black feminism

The three types of feminism discussed so far have all been criticised for ethnocentrism or assuming that the experiences of white women apply to all women.

Heidi Mirza argued that 'British feminism is still self-confidently all white' (Mirza, 1998), and that the needs of minority ethnic women are often ignored. Mirza further claims that myths about black women, such as the black superwoman who is assertive, confident and 'has it all', undermine attempts to make the real lives of black women better.

Key black feminists: Heidi Mirza, Bell Hooks, Sojourner Truth

Anti-feminism

Catherine Hakim has controversially claimed that the reason for a lack of equality is because of women's own choices to prioritise marriage and children over a career. She stated that many women are less committed to careers than men. Hakim claims that women's choosing to work part-time is an example of this.

However, Hakim's views have been heavily criticised; many women work part-time due to childcare responsibilities rather than their own choice. Men are parents too and are not so often faced with this 'choice'. The structure of society and unequal parental leave arrangements (in which women can currently take up to a year's maternity leave and men only two weeks) reinforce traditional gender roles.

For some people, feminism was important in the past, but is now a spent force. Post-feminism emphasises the idea that gender equality has been achieved and that feminism has had its day. However, there is much evidence that gender inequality remains; unequal pay is an example. While there is gender inequality, feminism will continue to be relevant. A quote from Meg Sullivan sums this up: 'I'll be post-feminist in the post-patriarchy.'

Think about ...

To find out more about contemporary feminism, visit the F Word website (http://www.thefword.org.uk).

See also:
Glass ceiling;
Patriarchy.

References

BRUEGEL, I. (1979) Women as a Reserve Army of Labour: A Note on Recent British Experience. *Feminist Review*. 3.

FIRESTONE, S. (1970) *The Dialectic of Sex*. New York: Farrar, Straus and Giroux.

MIRZA, H. (1998) All White Now. In COCHRANE, K. (ed.) (2012) *Women of the Revolution: Forty Years of Feminism*. London: Guardian Books.

ROWBOTHAM, S. (1989) *The Past is Before Us: Feminism in Action Since the 1960s*. London: Pandora.

Fordism

Fordism is a type of mass production created by Henry Ford, who founded the Ford Motor Company in America in the early 1900s. Fordism not only revolutionised the production of cars, making them available to the general population, but also changed the ways other goods were produced and led to significant changes in the workplace. The Fordist model has since been replicated in the mass production of many goods.

Characteristics of Fordism

➤ **Standardisation:** Products were made in a uniform way to the same specification. The Model T Ford was a very popular and simply designed car and Ford stated in his autobiography that the customer could buy it in any colour as long as it was black! (Ford, 1922)

➤ **Efficiency:** Ford was influenced by the efficiency model of Frederick Taylor, who increased the speed of workers so that more products could be produced and sold. Taylor timed workers with stopwatches and the other workers would copy the technique of whoever was fastest.

➤ **Assembly-line production:** The work was broken down into small parts. Rather than relying on skilled craftsmanship, almost any worker could be trained to do the same task over and over again. According to Marxists, this led to workers experiencing alienation; as they made the same part all day, they did not get the satisfaction of seeing a product through to its completed state and therefore felt detached from their work. Braverman claimed that Fordism led to deskilling as workers only needed to be trained in one skill to be used repetitively. (Fulcher & Scott, 2000)

➤ **Higher pay for workers:** As costs became lower with mass production, Ford could pay his workers more than was expected for factory workers of the time. This gave workers an incentive not to quit. Despite the use of more machinery, car manufacturing still involved heavy manual labour. The workers were motivated by higher wages together with a scheme to buy their own car (at the time, car ownership was only for the very wealthy), which in turn meant that Ford could sell more. Note that higher pay was not a reality for workers in all organisations; the perception that work was unskilled meant many factory owners felt justified in paying their workers less.

In many ways, Fordism marked the beginnings of a consumer society; the workers could now afford to pay for the products they made due to mass production driving down costs, which led to greater consumption and which, in turn, created more demand for production.

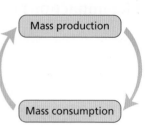

Post-Fordism

Fordism could not persist indefinitely because once a product had been bought by the masses, the market became saturated (Fulcher & Scott, 2000). If the product available to buy was always made to the same model, the consumer would only buy a new one once the old one had broken down. Today's consumer buys something new because they want **choice**. Brands continue to come up with new innovations to compete with others in the market. For example, many people will buy a new mobile phone whenever the latest model comes out, so the companies have to keep up with new technology.

Characteristics of post-Fordism

➤ **Choice:** Today's consumer expects a diversity of products to choose from to suit their different lifestyles and interests, buying products more frequently than a hundred years ago. Increasingly, consumers like to feel they are getting a unique niche product rather than a mass-produced product.

> **Flexible workers:** Rather than a division of labour in which workers perform one monotonous task, people are expected to multi-task and have a range of transferable skills which will be of use in a different organisation. This is particularly important in times of economic uncertainty as the idea of a job for life no longer applies.

The impact of Fordism today

Fordism has had a lasting legacy in society. Yiannis Gabriel (1988) notes that Fordism is still very relevant in catering; for example, fast food is made on a production line, often with one member of staff on each work station. Fast food is standardised with no variation across the different franchises. This appeals to many customers as they know what they will be getting before they buy it. However, often the sense that these are mass-produced goods is hidden in the idea that the consumer can have the food tailor-made to suit; for example, Burger King uses the slogan 'have it your way' to imply a wide range of options.

Think about ...

Research two businesses on the internet. How far do they follow Fordist or post-Fordist practices?

See also:
Consumerism;
Deskilling;
Marxism.

References

FORD, H. (1922) *My Life and Work*. New York: Doubleday Page.

FULCHER, J. & SCOTT, J. (2000) *Sociology*. Oxford: Oxford University Press.

GABRIEL, Y. (1988) *Working Lives in Catering*. London: Routledge and Kegan Paul.

Functionalism

Functionalism is a consensus theory, based on the idea that society needs agreement about norms and values to work effectively. Functionalists see society as being made up of many institutions, each contributing to the wellbeing of society as a whole. They have compared society to the human body. Key functionalists include Emile Durkheim, Talcott Parsons, and Robert Merton.

Durkheim

Functionalism is commonly associated with the work of Emile Durkheim. Writing in the late 1800s after the Industrial Revolution, he witnessed significant changes taking place in society; for example, he was interested in the move from mechanical to organic solidarity.

Before industrialisation, society was held together by social duty. People mostly lived in close-knit communities. Individualism was discouraged. There was a high level of collective consciousness. This was **mechanical solidarity**.

During and after industrialisation, the social cohesion that bonded individuals together was no longer about knowing each other, but was based on dependency in working relationships. People moved into towns and cities for work.

The division of labour means that individuals rely on each other for the goods and services they need. Sticking together for the good of the community has been replaced by an attitude of 'you scratch my back and I'll scratch yours'.

Durkheim is perhaps best known for his classic study *Suicide* (1897). Although suicide is regarded as a very personal act, Durkheim argued that it was not due to the personality of the individual alone but could be explained by social factors. He analysed suicide rates and found that suicide was most common when social integration and social regulation (rules) were either too high or too low. He identified four types of suicide.

	Low	High
Social integration	**Egoistic:** suicide resulting from excessive individualisation or lacking social support.	**Altruistic:** the needs of the community take precedence over the individual, e.g. suicide bombers.
Social regulation	**Anomic:** suicide resulting from a lack of clear norms due to changes in society and a loss of routine, e.g. due to redundancy or bankruptcy.	**Fatalistic:** (less common) the individual feels too much pressure from rules and regulations, e.g. the suicides of slaves and prisoners.

Durkheim argued that as there were patterns and trends, suicide rates needed to be seen as social facts. Social facts, unlike ideas, were measurable, observable and could be treated like objects in the natural sciences.

Parsons

Talcott Parsons argued that basic needs must be met so that social order and solidarity can be achieved. He called these needs 'functional prerequisites'. All social systems need to adhere to these four functional prerequisites:

1. **Adaptation:** This refers to the need of a social system to adapt to its environment to survive; for example, a family requires individual members to go out to work to provide food and shelter for the other members.

2. **Goal attainment:** Societies and institutions set goals towards which activities are directed; for example, a family sets a goal to save money for a holiday. This might involve everyone taking on extra work.

3. **Integration:** This refers to the need to maintain cohesion and avoid conflict. The family might have house rules and resolve disputes during a family meeting around the dinner table.

4. **Pattern maintenance:** This means ensuring that individual members are committed to the system as a whole and adopt routines. The family will socialise children to share common values.

Evaluation of functionalism

Strengths	Weaknesses
• Functionalists see the connection between the individual and society and also recognise the interdependence of institutions; for example, the family shapes the education system which in turn shapes the workplace. • It acknowledges that human behaviour is caused by society and that there are patterns in human behaviour – a crucial contribution to Sociology. • Functionalism accounts for change. Sometimes it is viewed as a conservative theory, but this is somewhat unfair; for example, Durkheim discussed change resulting from industrialisation.	• The existence of a value consensus in society has been challenged for two key reasons: ◊ Marxists claim that values have been imposed by the bourgeoisie rather than agreed. ◊ Since functionalists began writing, there has been a growth of cultural diversity due to mass immigration. This has led to a diversity of values (although arguably some core values are shared regardless of ethnicity, e.g. love and respect). • It ignores free will; postmodernists criticise functionalists for neglecting the choices individuals have. The organic analogy might not be appropriate as the organs of the body have no choice but to work together; yet the people who make up society's institutions do to an extent. • The theory overemphasises stability and seems out of line with society today which has seen instability from recession, riots, and strikes following public sector cuts.

Think about ...

Why is functionalism described as a consensus theory?

See also: Anomie; Organic analogy; Social facts; Warm bath theory.

References

DURKHEIM, E. (1997) *The Division of Labor in Society*. Introduction by COSER, L. A. New York: Free Press.

DURKHEIM, E. (1951) *Suicide*. New York: Free Press.

MERTON, R. (1957) *Social Theory and Social Structure*. New York: Free Press of Glencoe.

MORRISON, K. (1995) *Marx, Durkheim, Weber: Formations of Modern Social Thought*. London: Sage Publications.

PARSONS, T. *Today: His Theory and Legacy in Contemporary Sociology*. Edited by A. Javier Trevino. New York: Rowan & Littlefield, 2001.

Glass ceiling

The glass ceiling is a metaphor used to describe the invisible barrier preventing women from reaching the most senior levels of their occupations. As the ceiling is glass, women can see the senior jobs but society often presents obstacles that prevent them from climbing the corporate career ladder. Glass can, of course, be broken and some women are now chief executive officers (CEO) for major organisations.

Statistics

The BBC analysed a range of occupations and found that women hold fewer than a third of the 'top jobs' in the UK. According to the findings, women represent:

➤ 1.3 per cent of senior military ranks across the armed forces

➤ 13.2 per cent of the most senior judges

➤ 16.6 per cent of the most senior staff in the police. (Holt, 2012)

Women in the boardroom

A key concern that illustrates the glass ceiling in the UK is the lack of women executive directors of top companies. There have never been more than five women FTSE executives at any one time and, according to BoardWatch, none of the executives appointed to FTSE 100 boards* in 2012 were women. (Boardwatch, 2012)

* The FTSE 100 is made up of the 100 companies in the UK Stock Exchange with the biggest market value.

The following graph shows that in 2011 men considerably outnumbered women as board members in the EU. However, in Norway the gap was smaller than in other countries because the government had imposed a quota that at least 40 per cent of board members of listed companies should be women. The UK government has told FTSE 100 companies that at least a quarter of all directors must be women by 2015. (Sweigart, 2012; Ginsberg, 2011)

Board members in the top companies in the European Union

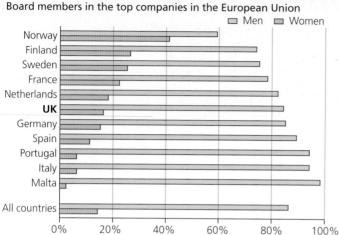

Based on *Women in economic decision-making in the EU: Progress report, A Europe 2020*, Fig.1, p.9

The underrepresentation of women in the boardroom indicates that the glass ceiling concept is still highly relevant in contemporary society.

Explanations for a glass ceiling

1. **'Old boys' network':** Social and business connections of former pupils from prestigious male-only public schools are closed off to women. Through an informal network, men might be encouraged to apply for certain elite positions, thereby excluding women.

2. **Confidence:** The term 'glass ceiling' may in itself be unhelpful and self-perpetuating. Knowledge of barriers might reduce women's confidence and discourage them from applying for top positions. A survey in 2011 of 3,000 members of the Institute of Leadership and Management found that 73 per cent of female respondents believed that barriers still existed for women aiming to have board-level positions.

3. **Pregnancy and motherhood:** The UK's parental leave laws are very unequal; at the time of publication, women take up to a year's maternity leave, whereas

men are only entitled to two weeks' paternity leave. This law reinforces traditional conjugal roles. Board-level positions are normally seen as very inflexible and difficult to access for women due to childcare. The feminist writer Rosie Boycott explains: 'We tell girls to reach for the stars as they're growing up, only to tell them to reach for the door the moment they reproduce.' (Boycott, 2008)

Think about ...

What are the main arguments in favour of and against using quotas to increase the representation of women?

See also: Patriarchy.

References

BOARDWATCH (2012) *Women on Boards*. [Online] Available from: http://www.boardsforum.co.uk/boardwatch.html. [Accessed: 27th January 2013].

BOYCOTT, R. (2008) The world is still organised to meet the wishes of men. *The Guardian*. 28th February. [Online] Available from: http://www.guardian.co.uk/commentisfree/2008/feb/28/gender. [Accessed: 27th January 2013].

GINSBERG, J. (2011) FTSE 100 should aim for 25 per cent female boards. *Reuters*. 24th February. [Online] Available from: http://uk.reuters.com/article/2011/02/24/uk-britain-directors-women-idUKTRE71N0TN20110224. [Accessed: 27th February 2013].

HOLT, G. (2012) Women hold fewer than a third of top jobs – BBC research. *BBC News*. 29th May. [Online] Available from: http://www.bbc.co.uk/news/uk-18187449. [Accessed: 27th January 2013].

INSTITUTE OF LEADERSHIP AND MANAGEMENT (2011) Ambition and Gender at Work. [Online] Available from: http://www.i-l-m.com/downloads/resources/centres/communications-and-marketing/ILM_Ambition_and_Gender_report_0211. [Accessed: 27th January 2013].

SWEIGART, A. (2012) Women on Board for Change: The Norway Model of Boardroom Quotas as a Tool For Progress in the United States and Canada. *Northwestern Journal of International Law & Business*. 32 (4). [Online] Available from: http://scholarlycommons.law.northwestern.edu/cgi/viewcontent. [Accessed: 27th January 2013].

Globalisation

Globalisation refers to the increasing interdependence of the different countries throughout the world. The cultural, economic and political connections that different countries have with each other enable citizens to see the world as a single place where experiences are shared, and as a result different parts of the world feel less 'foreign'. However, inequalities of wealth and poverty remain, and these inequalities are arguably worsened by globalisation.

The causes of globalisation

1 The mass media and global communication

Through the development of the mass media, it is now possible for people to know as much about what is happening on the other side of the world as about their own country. Hundreds of years ago the English did not know that the Americas existed, and one hundred years ago news from North America could take weeks to reach England by letter or by telegram, yet we knew about 9/11 as it happened; it was 'breaking news'.

This growth of global communication has been particularly noticeable since the introduction of social networking sites such as Facebook, which connects over a billion users across the world. In this sense, the world is theoretically shrinking to become a 'global village'.

2 Changes in work and the economy

Today, in a largely deindustrialised society, there is increasing international competition in order to make a profit. There has been a rise in the numbers of Transnational Corporations – organisations which market their products across the world. Examples include Apple, Sony and Nike. The UK's economy is closely linked to that of other countries; for example, the recession of 2008 was due to a global banking crisis.

The World Trade Organization has broken down barriers between different countries by promoting free trade.

However, this trade is not always fair; in countries such as India and Malaysia, labour costs are lower, so many Western companies' products are made in poorer countries to improve profits, resulting in workers being exploited by working long hours for low pay. The use of the term 'third world' makes developing countries seem very distanced and removed from Western culture, as though they are 'not our problem', but through unfair trade they have arguably been driven into debt by Western countries.

3   The growth of travel

Before the 1960s, very few working-class British people went on holiday overseas and air travel was only for the rich. Today budget airlines have opened up the world to more people. With improved technology, it is now quicker to see different parts of the world by train and plane.

4   International politics

The UK is increasingly connected to other countries politically. It is a member of the United Nations (UN), which aims to protect human rights and to achieve world peace. It is also a member of the North Atlantic Treaty Organization (NATO) through which member countries agree to help each other if any one country is attacked. Since 1994, the UK has had greater connections with Europe due to joining the European Union (the EU).

Global culture

Due to globalisation, the day-to-day cultural experiences of individuals across the world are becoming more homogenous (similar). Imagine a day in the life of a retail worker: she wakes up and checks Facebook, then visits Starbucks for a coffee on the way to work; she buys her lunch from McDonald's and a pair of trainers from a Nike store; once home, she watches *The Simpsons* on TV before meeting friends to watch the latest Hollywood blockbuster.

Whether she comes from the UK, America, Japan or Russia, she could have this same cultural experience.

Loss of national culture

A possible consequence of globalisation is the weakening of national and regional identities. Traditional ideas start to be questioned. Anthony Giddens refers to this as detraditionalisation. Some individuals try to resist a global identity by celebrating British traditions and buying British locally-sourced products; there has been a growing popularity of farmers' markets, for example.

For Giddens (cited in Thompson, 2009), there is a positive aspect which he referred to as 'cosmopolitanism'. This means that individuals are less restricted by traditions than they were pre-globalisation, and so have more freedom to live as they want to. They have greater choices regarding how they conduct their relationships, where they shop, what they do for entertainment and how they exercise political power. Culture becomes more fluid.

Think about ...

Look at the labels in your clothes. Where were they made? What do these countries have in common? Why do British companies have clothes manufactured in countries that are hundreds of miles away?

See also:
Consumer culture; Culture; Hybridity.

Reference

THOMPSON, K. (2009) Globalisation, Culture and Identity. *Sociology Review.* 18 (4).

Habitus

Habitus is a concept introduced by Pierre Bourdieu to refer to the values, social roles, dispositions and tastes that individuals or social groups have because of their life experiences. The environment individuals are surrounded by influences their behaviour. Many forms of behaviour become habitual and taken for granted; they become habits. They are regulated without needing to adhere to rules, in a largely unthinking way. Bourdieu called this the logic of practice.

The habitus, background and culture

Habitus can also be seen as the resources people have at their disposal to get along in society. These include their language, accent, dress, manners and social class. Derek Layder states that Bourdieu's ideas of the habitus refer to the knowledge an individual possesses because of their background. Their background or culture will influence their use of language, experiences of education, attitudes towards marriage and parenting, career aspirations and much more (Layder, 2000). The individual may not be aware of this influence.

The habitus, social class and the body

Bourdieu argued that people's bodies bear the imprint of their class and determine their identity: 'What is learned by the body is not something that one has...but something that one is' (Bourdieu, 1990). This includes their mannerisms, the way they dress, the food they eat and even the sports they play (Bourdieu, 1984). Bourdieu claimed that the sports typically practised by the middle classes tended to focus on posture, restraint and discipline (for example ballet, fencing and horse riding), whereas for the working classes, sports typically focused on higher levels of pain and physical exertion (for example boxing, football). The working classes are at a disadvantage because the activities they take part in give them less chance to convert their physical capital into cultural capital. The middle class as the dominant class gets to determine what activities are important for society. (Shilling, 2012)

The habitus and taste

Cultural capital depends on taste, and taste is acquired by the habitus (Bourdieu, 1984). For Bourdieu, taste is not individualistic; it is socially influenced. The working class might have tastes of necessity which are defined negatively, whereas the middle class might have tastes of luxury or refined tastes because they have more freedom of choice and such tastes are defined positively by society. (Consider the status of high culture compared to popular culture.)

Criticisms of the habitus concept

A criticism of Bourdieu's work is that, in stating that individuals are conditioned by the habitus, it neglects the idea that individuals have free will to change. Bourdieu assumes that the habitus predisposes an individual towards certain types of behaviour, but individuals can also be creative. Also, if the working class tries to copy middle-class lifestyles, that is a conscious act and brings into question Bourdieu's claim that the habitus operates below the level of consciousness.

Think about ...

What assumptions do people make based on the appearance of others?

See also:
Agency and structure;
Capital;
Socialisation.

References

BOURDIEU, P. (1984) *Distinction: A Social Critique of the Judgement of Taste*. London: Routledge.

BOURDIEU, P. (1977) *Outline of a Theory of Practice*. Cambridge: Cambridge University Press.

BOURDIEU, P. (1990) *The Logic of Practice*. Cambridge: Polity Press.

LAYDER, D. (2000) *Understanding Social Theory*. London: Sage Publications.

SHILLING, C. (2012) *The Body and Social Theory*. London: Sage Publications.

Hidden curriculum

The hidden curriculum is a concept which was first used by Philip Jackson in *Life in Classrooms* (1968). It describes all the learning which takes place in school that is not taught as part of the formal or national curriculum. As well as maths and English, children also learn about how to behave, what will be expected in the workplace and the structure of society.

Examples of the hidden curriculum

Preparation for the workplace

➤ **Time keeping:** Most schools use bells to ensure lessons run on time. Excellent punctuality and attendance are rewarded with certificates, while those who arrive late might be given a detention, just as employees who frequently arrive late to work may be subject to disciplinary action.

➤ **Obedience:** Children learn to obey through a system of rewards (such as merit points) and sanctions (such as detentions). This relates to the workplace where the employee is expected to follow orders.

Messages about the wider society

➤ Many children in lower ability sets are from working-class backgrounds, while top sets are dominated by middle-class children. What might this say about perceived ability and relative power in society?

➤ Black male children in the UK have the highest rate of permanent exclusions from schools. In 2009–2010, four fifths of permanent exclusions were boys and African Caribbean children's rate of exclusion was four times higher than that of white children. This relates to the wider society in which African Caribbeans are overrepresented in prisons. Is this an example of racism in society?

Ivan Illich

Ivan Illich argued that schools teach children an uncritical acceptance of inequality – that their role in life is 'to know their place and sit still in it'. In his 1973 book *Deschooling Society*, Illich proposed a radical departure from the current education system to one based on freedom and creative learning where children and adults can learn (through lifelong learning), acting on their own initiative.

Functionalist and Marxist perspectives

According to functionalists, the hidden curriculum is important because it teaches children skills that are needed in society. They believe that it is a fair or meritocratic system because children are rewarded for 'good' behaviour which is important for the smooth running of a school and later for the wider society. However, Marxists Samuel Bowles and Herbert Gintis believe that it teaches children to accept a ruling class ideology that benefits the bourgeoisie.

Think about ...

Do you agree more with the functionalist or Marxist perspective of the hidden curriculum?

See also:
Correspondence principle;
Functionalism;
Marxism;
Meritocracy.

References

BOWLES, S. & GINTIS, H. (1976) *Schooling in Capitalist America*. London: Routledge and Kegan Paul.

ILLICH, I. (1973) *Deschooling Society*. Harmondsworth: Penguin Education.

POVERTY SITE (2011) School exclusions. [Online] Available from: http://www.poverty.org.uk/27/index.shtml. [Accessed: 1st March 2013].

PRISON REFORM TRUST (2012) Bromley Briefings Prison Factfile. [Online] Available from: http://www.prisonreformtrust.org.uk/Portals/0/Documents/FactfileJune2012. [Accessed: 1st March 2013].

Hybridity

In a sociological context, the term hybridity is used to describe a mixture or fusion of cultural influences. The term is very relevant to the UK today, particularly in its cities which are culturally diverse and have been so since the mass immigration of the 1960s. Even areas of the UK that have experienced very little immigration are still shaped by cultural hybridity due to globalisation and media influences.

Influences on hybrid identities

A major influence on the shaping of hybrid identities has been the rise in dual heritage or mixed-race births. There was no dual heritage option on the Census until 2001, yet by 2009 it had become the fastest growing ethnic group in the UK. In Leicester, there are more mixed-race births than Asian births and nationally one in ten children is part of a mixed-race family. (BBC, 2009)

Hybridity also applies to second and third generation minority ethnic groups who experience a fusion of 'home' culture of their parents or grandparents and British culture. Hybridity has also shaped the culture and identity of Britons as a whole as shown in this table.

Examples of hybridity

Food	Food in Britain today is influenced by cultures from around the world. Chicken tikka masala is considered Britain's favourite dish. It is a good example of a cultural hybrid because while the chicken tikka is Indian, the masala sauce was added as a result of the influence of traditional British meals with meat and gravy.
Music	In the 1990s, Asian music was absorbed into British mainstream popular culture through the fusion of British and Asian influences dubbed as 'Brasian'. Examples of bands included Cornershop and Babylon Zoo. More recently, the music of Barbadian singer Rihanna has mixed mainstream American pop and RnB with Bajan Creole language.

Hybridity: a focus on language

Hundreds of different languages are spoken in the UK today and in multicultural cities new forms of hybrid languages have developed.

Hinglish

Hinglish is a hybrid of Hindi and English. It has for some time been an important language in India where English had previously been the main language used in the world of work. Baljinder Mahal, author of the Hinglish dictionary *The Queen's Hinglish*, observes that the language is now also spoken in many homes and multicultural school playgrounds in the UK.

According to Mahal, changes in language reflect changes in identities. She argues that individuals are not expected to have one fixed identity and the same should therefore be true of the languages they speak. (Mahal, 2008)

Examples of Hinglish phrases:

badmash = hooligan; airdash = being in a hurry; innit = isn't it.

Multicultural London English

Multicultural London English is a dialect that emerged in the East End of London but is now used by many young people throughout the cities of the UK. It contains a mixture of Caribbean languages (particularly patois) and South Asian languages. The East End of London is very culturally diverse with areas where non-white people outnumber white. Therefore, some immigrants to the UK are learning English informally from other immigrant groups rather than native speakers. In addition, the white young people living in these areas will often have culturally diverse friendship groups which have caused new variations of language to emerge.

Examples of Multicultural London English phrases:

endz = neighbourhood; bare = lots;
wasteman = an idiot or loser;
allow it = let it be/leave something alone.

The use of Multicultural London English has been dubbed 'Jafaican' but the accusation of trying to copy Jamaicans or 'trying to be black' is incorrect according to Sue Fox (cited in *The Independent*, 2006). She claims that the reason young people are using the dialect is because they have grown up around other young people from diverse backgrounds and therefore share culture. The dialect is authentic to them.

Think about ...

Watch an episode of *EastEnders*. Can you identify examples of Multicultural London English used? How does this compare to the use of traditional East End cockney in the programme?

See also: Culture; Globalisation; Multiculturalism.

References

BBC (2009) The BBC talks to the mixed race community in Leicester. *Inside Out*. 13th November. [Online] Available from: http://news.bbc.co.uk/local/leicester/hi/people_and_places/newsid_8354000/8354830.stm. [Accessed: 7th February 2013].

COUGHLIN, S. (2006) It's Hinglish, innit? *BBC News Magazine*. 8th November. [Online] Available from: http://news.bbc.co.uk/1/hi/magazine/6122072.stm. [Accessed: 9th February 2013].

THE INDEPENDENT (2006) From the mouths of teens. 5th November. [Online] Available from: http://www.independent.co.uk/news/uk/this-britain/from-the-mouths-of-teens-422688.html. [Accessed: 9th February 2013].

Identity

Identity means a sense of self. It is how individuals see themselves and how they are seen by others. A sense of self is one of the things that makes us human. Jeffrey Weeks claimed that 'identity is about belonging, about what you have in common with some people and what differentiates you from others'. (1991)

CAGE

Identities are formed around belonging to different groups in society. The most significant of these are Class, Age, Gender and Ethnicity (CAGE).

Class

This is an identity based on social background and occupation. It is difficult to define the concept of class. For some, terms such as 'working class' and 'middle class' have less meaning than they did in the past, and postmodernists argue that we live in a classless society. For Jan Pakulski and Malcolm Waters, class is dead as a marker of identity.

There has been a growth of individualism in society with people feeling unique rather than having a group belonging. However, class is still a considerable source of inequality in society.

Age

Young children often tell people their age very precisely ('I am six and a half') because it is an important part of how they see themselves. Age is a socially constructed identity and the meanings attached to different life stages vary across cultures.

Many individuals have expectations of where they want to be by a certain age. Others try to be less fixated on age as a source of identity, but this is difficult in a society where youth is highly valued.

Gender

People are taught their gender identities from a very young age. The traits of being masculine or feminine are learned through the agents of socialisation; for example, parents tend to encourage their children to associate with their gender through their toys, such as dolls for girls and soldiers for boys. As a result, according to Paul Statham (1986), by the age of five, most children have rigid ideas about what is acceptable for boys and for girls.

Ethnicity

This is an identity based on shared cultural heritage. Members of the same ethnic group tend to speak the same language, share traditions and celebrations, and have a shared history and common descent.

It is a common mistake to assume that only minority groups have ethnicity (probably due to describing multicultural areas as 'ethnic'). Everyone has an ethnic identity, including white English people. Many people have dual or multiple ethnic identities and might 'code switch' from one to another; for example, Muhammad Anwar (1998) found that for South Asian girls there was pressure from the extended family to dress modestly in traditional Asian clothing, but many would wear Western clothing in order to fit in with their friends.

The CAGE groups are common markers of identity and it is important to stress the intersection of these sources of identity; for example, a middle-aged black woman might feel a more shared identity with a middle-aged white woman than with a young black man. There are many other factors which shape identity. These include sexuality, religion, political beliefs, nationality and regionality, leisure activities, and even the football team supported can be a strong factor in the way individuals see themselves.

The 'looking-glass self'

The 'looking-glass self' is a concept that was coined by Charles Cooley. He stated that an individual's sense of self is shaped by their perceptions of how others see them. Metaphorically, the individual holds a mirror up to themselves to imagine how others judge their appearance and behaviour, and then a sense of self is developed through the perceived judgements of others. As social beings, we seek the approval of others in the formation of our identities.

Think about ...

Write down the first five characteristics that come to mind about your own identity. What is at the top of your list? What does your list reveal about the way you see yourself?

See also:
Culture;
Femininities;
Hybridity;
Masculinities;
Social class;
Socialisation.

References

ANWAR, M. (1998) *Between Cultures: Continuity and Change in the Lives of Young Asians*. London: Routledge.

COOLEY, C. H. (1956) *The Two Major Works of Charles H. Cooley: Social Organization; Human Nature and the Social Order*. Free Press.

WEEKS, J. (1991) *Against Nature: Essays on History, Sexuality and Identity*. London: Rivers Oram Press.

Institutional racism

While individual racism can be defined as hatred or deliberate discrimination shown by one individual to another because of their race, institutional racism operates on a wider societal level. It can be more subtle, and arguably includes the unintended exclusion of others.

Institutional racism has been defined as: 'The collective failure of an organisation to provide an appropriate and professional service to people because of their colour, culture or ethnic origin. It can be seen or detected in processes, attitudes and behaviour which amount to discrimination through unwitting prejudice, ignorance, thoughtlessness and racist stereotyping which disadvantage minority ethnic people.' (Macpherson, 1999)

The term 'institutional racism' entered the public's consciousness when used by Judge Sir William Macpherson, the chair of the official inquiry into the murder of Stephen Lawrence. Although the main focus of the inquiry was on the police, the report suggested that all major organisations in Britain are characterised by institutional racism. (Parekh, 2000, cited in Pilkington, 2003)

The Stephen Lawrence Inquiry

Stephen Lawrence was an 18-year-old student stabbed to death in a racially motivated attack by five men in 1993. Macpherson accused the police involved of institutional racism. They were criticised for not immediately searching for witnesses. Lawrence's friends reported being asked irrelevant questions about whether they were in gangs rather than the facts of what happened that night. The failure to make early arrests led to a lack of evidence which meant that the case collapsed

twice. It took over 18 years for two of the killers to be convicted of the murder.

Further examples of institutional racism

Adoption
In 2009–2010, black children took on average over 50 per cent longer to be placed for adoption than children from other ethnic groups (Department for Education, 2011). This may be partly due to the attempt to match the ethnicity of the child with that of the adoptive parents. While white adults can adopt black and other minority ethnic children, the attempt to get a 'perfect match' can leave children in the care system for longer.

Education
David Gillborn has argued that some people incorrectly think that the battle against institutional racism has been won and that the mass media have turned their focus onto the white working class as the new race 'victims'. For Gillborn, this is mistaken as Caribbean students are still less likely to attain five good GCSEs than other ethnic groups and are more likely to be permanently excluded from school. (Gillborn, 2008)

Police stop and search
Research by the Equality and Human Rights Commission (EHRC) shows that police forces in the West Midlands are up to 28 times more likely to use stop-and-search powers against black people than white people. Simon Woolley, a commissioner at the EHRC, said that nationally black youths are still being disproportionately targeted (cited in Dodd, 2012).

Attempts to eradicate institutional racism

The Stephen Lawrence Inquiry left a legacy that changed race relations in Britain. One example originating from the inquiry was the Race Relations Amendment Act in 2000, which was designed to outlaw race discrimination in all public functions and to state the need for public, private and voluntary organisations to be proactive in challenging racial discrimination.

Following the Equality Act of 2010, employers are allowed to use positive action to prevent the disadvantage of minority ethnic groups. This means that they can choose to hire candidates from underrepresented groups provided they are as qualified for the role as other applicants. This should not be confused with positive discrimination where a candidate would be chosen *because* they are from a minority ethnic group (this is unlawful).

Think about ...

What steps should be taken to prevent institutional racism in education?

See also:
Ethnocentrism.

References

BBC NEWS (2004) Rise in police searches of Asians. 2nd July. [Online] Available from: http://news.bbc.co.uk/1/hi/uk/3859023.stm. [Accessed: 4th January 2013].

DEPARTMENT FOR EDUCATION (2011) Government to look at strengthening inspection of LA adoption services. [Online] Available from: http://www.education.gov.uk/inthenews/inthenews/a0074754/breaking-down-barriers-to-adoption. [Accessed: 4th January 2013].

DODD, V. (2012) Police up to 28 times more likely to stop and search black people. *The Guardian*. 12th June. [Online] Available from: http://www.guardian.co.uk/uk/2012/jun/12/police-stop-and-search-black-people. [Accessed: 4th January 2013].

GILLBORN, D. *Racism and Education: Coincidence or Conspiracy?* London: Routledge.

MACPHERSON, W. (1999) *The Stephen Lawrence Inquiry: Report of an Inquiry by Sir William Macpherson of Cluny.* London: The Stationery Office.

PILKINGTON, A. (2003) *Racial Disadvantage and Ethnic Diversity in Britain.* Basingstoke: Palgrave Macmillan.

Interpretivism

Interpretivism is an alternative sociological perspective to **positivism**. Unlike positivists, interpretivists do not believe that we can apply a scientific method to studying people. For interpretivists, the focus is looking for the meanings behind social actions and how we then construct our social world by attaching these meanings to different situations.

Which methods do interpretivists prefer?

An interpretivist approach favours the collection of qualitative data to gain knowledge of the feelings and experiences of individuals rather than larger-scale generalisations based on quantitative research. Methods include:

Unstructured interviews

➤ This method produces valid data giving insight into people's experiences and the meanings they attach to them.

➤ The interviewer can build a rapport and use empathy to interpret the data.

➤ The unstructured nature of the interviews allows flexibility, so the researcher can ask follow-up questions to gain deeper understandings.

Participant and non-participant observation

➤ Observation enables the researcher to either overtly or covertly observe behaviours in the natural environment. This means they can gather qualitative, valid data.

➤ However, covert research may be affected by the Hawthorne effect, where subjects behave differently because they know they are being studied.

Max Weber explains Sociology as a science which tries to interpret and explain social action in order to understand its effects. For interpretivists, it is the process of 'interpreting understandings' which is crucial. This directly contrasts with the positivist approach of discovering social facts which are external forces acting on the individual and shaping their behaviours (cited in Bryman, 2012). Weber uses the term 'Verstehen' (meaning 'understanding') to illustrate this idea.

It is important that social research involves a true understanding of the subject; for example, using participant observation to increase empathy and become an 'insider' in terms of the social experience.

Social action

This sociological approach was founded by Weber, who maintained that an understanding of both social structures and social actions are necessary to gain a full knowledge of human behaviour. In a social action approach, there are two levels of understanding to be investigated:

➤ the cause of actions: this refers to structures in society that may shape a person's behaviour, for example social class

➤ the meaning of actions: this refers to the subjective meanings people attach to their actions on an individual level.

Through acquiring knowledge of both these levels, the social researcher can gain Verstehen.

Case study: Janet Foster

Foster (1995) conducted a study using participant observations and semi-structured interviews on the Riverside estate in East London. Official statistics indicated high levels of crime in the area; however, through her research, Foster found that the perceptions of local residents were quite different. They felt that the area wasn't one of particularly high crime due to 'informal social control'; in other words, the way they behaved towards each other allowed the community to feel generally safe and secure. One interviewee said, 'I feel quite safe because you know your neighbours and you know they're there…they look out for you.' Others mentioned how if they hear or see disturbances, they 'don't stand for it' and they call the police.

Foster's study demonstrates how, by using interpretivist methods of collecting qualitative data, the researcher can gain valid results. In this case, the official statistics alone would have revealed something quite different, that is, 'social facts', which did not accurately portray the perceptions of Riverside's people.

Think about …

List the strengths and weaknesses of an interpretivist approach to sociological research.

See also:
Positivism;
Qualitative data;
Quantitative data; Social facts; Verstehen; Weberianism.

References

BRYMAN, A. (2012) *Social Research Methods*. 4th Ed. Oxford: Oxford University Press.

FOSTER, J. (1995) Informal Social Control and Community Crime Prevention. *British Journal of Criminology*. 35 (4). p.563–583.

WEBB, R., WESTERGAARD, H., TROBE, K. & STEEL, L. (2009) *A2 Sociology*. Brentwood: Napier Press.

Left and right realism

The realist approach towards crime emerged in the 1970s and 1980s when thinking shifted towards the idea that the source of lawlessness is within the individual rather than the fabric of society. During this period, New Right governments were in power, both in the UK with Thatcher and in the USA with Reagan. These governments favoured a tough stance on crime and influenced the thinking of realists.

The realist perspective on crime

Realists maintain that there has been a rise in crime rates, as well as a rise in concern for the fear of crime in society and the impact on victims. They advocate the necessity for practical policies to reduce crime. (Webb et al, 2009)

Right realism

Right realists share the neo-conservative outlook of the governments of the 1980s and recognise the need for strict law and order policies. They support punishments with the purposes of retribution and deterrence from crime, as well as being a means of getting criminals off the streets. This 'zero tolerance' approach is designed to decrease public fear rather than to rehabilitate criminals.

James Q. Wilson, one of the main right realist theorists, argues that crime is not the result of social factors as Marxism would maintain, but comes from factors within the individual. The main factors are:

1. **Biology:** Wilson believes that some individuals have the predisposition to commit crime, for example through personality traits such as aggression.

2. **Socialisation:** Right realists believe that effective socialisation is key to explaining crime as it is through the socialisation process that we learn morals and self-control. Right realists maintain that the ideal socialisation agency is the nuclear family.

3. **Choice:** Ronald Clarke believes that committing crime is based on a rational choice where the offender weighs up the likely consequences. Right realists maintain that, unless the justice system becomes less lenient, the 'cost' of crime will be perceived to be lower than the possible rewards as punishments may not be harsh enough to deter the criminal.

Criticisms of right realism

➤ It ignores structural causes of crime such as poverty.

➤ A 'zero tolerance' system in policing could perhaps heighten opportunities for police discrimination.

➤ Right realists, with their focus on retribution, fail to acknowledge instances where punishment has reformed offenders.

Left realism

Left realism developed since the 1980s as a response to the need to take the rising crime rate seriously and look for practical solutions. Left realists agree with Marxists in the belief that society is driven by capitalist forces and as such is unequal. However, they advocate gradual social change rather than a revolution. In terms of crime, this means developing explanations and practical strategies 'to address the problems as people experience them' (Hermida). They argue that crime must be taken seriously in terms of the impact on victims, for example women are afraid to go out at night for fear of attack.

Jock Young developed the left realist approach and, as a result, he suggests explanations for the rising crime rates.

1. **Relative deprivation:** Relative deprivation in this context refers to how deprived someone feels in relation to others; for example, feeling resentment

towards those who have more material wealth can lead to crime. Young claims that, particularly with the influence of advertising, people may resort to crime to acquire what they want. Relative deprivation can therefore occur anywhere in the social structure, which may help explain corporate crime as well as shoplifting.

2. **Marginalisation:** Some groups, such as unemployed youth, are marginalised in society and have little means of using political power to solve their problems. As a result, some might turn to street crime to vent their frustrations with society. (Webb et al, 2009)

Left realists propose that the police improve relations with local communities in order to increase trust; for example, using deterrence strategies in working-class neighbourhoods to prevent crime, rather than a large-scale police presence after an incident.

Criticisms of left realism

➤ A firmer approach may be necessary to be a real deterrent for potential criminals.

➤ Deprivation is not the only cause of crime, as many people face deprivation and never commit a deviant act.

Think about ...

Do you favour the left or right realist approach?

See also: Canteen culture.

References

HERRNSTEIN, R. & MURRAY, C. (1994) *The Bell Curve: Intelligence and Class Structure in American Life.* New York: Free Press.

WEBB, R., WESTERGAARD, H., TROBE, K. & STEEL, L. (2009) *A2 Sociology.* Brentwood: Napier Press.

YOUNG, J. (1992) Ten Points of Realism. In JEWKES, Y. & LETHERBY, J. (eds.) (2002) *Criminology: A Reader.* London: Sage Publications.

Life chances

Max Weber used the term 'life chances' to describe an individual's opportunities to gain access to material goods, services and cultural experiences – their likelihood of having a good quality of life. A person's position in society determines their prospects for 'good' life chances. Overall, the middle classes have better life chances than the working classes, with higher levels of education, more money and better health.

What determines life chances?

➤ **Inherited characteristics** – levels of wealth and social class position determined by the family

➤ **Level and duration of poverty** – child and family poverty (how many generations of the family have been in poverty), income and material deprivation

➤ **Parental and family influence** – family size, aspirations, values, parental interest/neglect, drug and alcohol addiction

➤ **Area** – housing, facilities, social networks, community, physical environment, access to local services, crime

➤ **Social and economic factors** – discrimination, strength of the economy (recession), employment opportunities

➤ **Policy intervention** – the effectiveness of social services working with children, families, vulnerable groups.

(Fabian Society, 2005)

Life chances and social class

While some people can overcome disadvantaged family backgrounds, there is a vicious cycle for others in which child poverty leads to ill health, low levels of education and poverty in adulthood. Children who grow up in poverty tend to continue to experience poverty as parents. (Fabian Society, 2005)

Education is a fundamental way of improving life chances. However, social class is the biggest deciding factor of educational success in the UK, where the attainment gap between students of different social classes is wider than in most developed countries in the world. In 2010–2011, just over a third of students who had free school meals achieved five or more GCSEs grade A*–C compared to nearly 60 per cent of students as a whole. (*The Guardian*, 2012)

Many strategies have been put in place to improve life chances, such as Sure Start centres designed to give children in deprived areas the best start in life. However, from 2013 a benefits cap means many people's benefits will go down. There is concern that this will have an adverse effect on life chances.

Think about ...

How can the life chances of children in poverty be improved?

See also:
Capital; Poverty;
Social mobility;
Underclass.

References

FABIAN SOCIETY (2006) *Narrowing the Gap: The Final Report of the Fabian Commission on Life Chances and Child Poverty.* London: Fabian Society.

THE GUARDIAN (2012) GCSE results 2010/11: by ethnicity, free school meals and first language. 10th February. [Online] Available from: http://www.guardian.co.uk/news/datablog/2012/feb/10/gcse-results-ethnicity-school-meals. [Accessed: 2nd February 2013].

Marketisation of education

The marketisation of education refers to the application of business principles to the education system. Just as shops compete for customers in a free market, so schools and colleges compete for students in an education market. Market principles were introduced into the education system by the New Right government of the 1980s. Many of the policies remain in place today.

Examples of marketisation

Examples include glossy college prospectuses featuring a 'menu' of subject choices, websites and social networking sites informing prospective students of events in the school, and open days where teachers try to 'sell' their subjects.

The 1988 Education Reform Act

Margaret Thatcher's New Right government implemented the 1988 Education Reform Act to increase competition between schools. They believed that such competition would raise standards as schools that were perceived to be underachieving would lose students, lose funding and ultimately face the threat of closing. This was a catalyst for change that moved away from the comprehensive principle that had been a key education policy since 1965. Key changes were:

➤ **The National Curriculum:** If schools were to compete, it had to be on equal terms with the same curriculum.

➤ **SATs:** Students had to sit Standard Attainment Tests at 7, 11 and 14 years of age. SATs were designed to measure the performance of schools.

➤ **League tables:** The results of SATs, as well as GCSEs and A levels, were published in league tables. Parents could then make a choice of school based on results.

Marketisation since the 1988 Act

The Labour government from 1997–2010 largely continued with the marketisation of education:

➤ League tables were now a fairer reflection of the school's performance as they included value-added data. This compared the performance of the student when starting school with their performance upon leaving; if a student starts secondary school with low SATs results but then achieves good GCSEs, the school is said to have 'added value' to that student.

➤ New Labour introduced academies: these were schools deemed to be failing which were taken over by local government with sponsorship from private businesses.

➤ There was an expansion of specialist schools as the government wanted to offer a range of choices rather than a 'one size fits all' school system.

The coalition government elected in 2010 went further, introducing free schools which are paid for by the state, but not controlled by the local authority. Parents can apply to set up a free school as long as they can prove there is demand and follow the National Curriculum.

The impact of market principles

Following the publication of results in league tables, parents (the middle class in particular) do whatever they can to get their child into the 'best school', including moving house. The schools become oversubscribed, adding to their appeal. Results are likely to continue to improve, attracting more students, and the cycle continues. However, schools with poorer results in league tables struggle to attract students, they become undersubscribed, lose funding and tend to suffer from a high turnover of teachers. Middle-class parents avoid sending their children there and so a two-tier system of state schools is created.

Evaluation of market principles

Strengths
➤ Accountability – the publication of league tables makes schools more accountable to the public and the taxpayer.

➤ Parentocracy – parents can make informed choices of where to send their children based on league tables.

➤ A national curriculum arguably creates equal opportunities as students learn the same core content.

Weaknesses
➤ Parental choice is often limited to choice for the middle class who may be in a better position to move house to get their child into a 'good school'.

➤ Market principles represent a move away from comprehensive principles of equal opportunities.

➤ A focus on marketing takes time away from teaching.

➤ Andy Hargreaves (1995) criticised the adoption of business principles; he stated that we now have a Kentucky Fried education system of franchises. Schools have students, not units, but much of the literature on education management does not reflect this.

Think about ...

Look at a school prospectus. What strategies are used to encourage students to enrol?

See also:
Hidden
curriculum.

Reference

HARGREAVES, A. (1995) Kentucky Fried Schooling? *Times Educational Supplement*. 31st March.

Marxism

Marxism is the philosophy developed by Karl Marx and Friedrich Engels in the 1800s. Although Marxism has its origins in politics and economics, Marx is widely regarded as one of the founding fathers of Sociology and one of the most influential sociological thinkers of all time. Marxism is a conflict theory based on the idea that there is inequality in society between the ruling class (the **bourgeoisie**) and the working class (the **proletariat**).

Historical materialism

Marx used the term 'historical materialism' to stress that throughout history, human beings have had to put survival ahead of anything else. The ways in which people provide for their basic necessities in life shapes their social relations.

Marx and Engels stated in their book *The Communist Manifesto* (1848) that 'the history of all hitherto existing society is the history of class struggles'. (Marx & Engels,1848)

Marxists state that it is **economic production** which shapes the social world, and for the proletariat their means of survival was to work for the bourgeoisie despite exploitation. Note that Marx identified a third class between the bourgeoisie and the proletariat called the 'petite bourgeoisie'. An example is small shop owners. However, as they did not own a large means of production, Marx considered them to be less significant in the class struggle.

Exploitation by the bourgeoisie

Marxists see capitalism (the economic system based on the private ownership of wealth) as an exploitative system in which the bourgeoisie own the means of production (the things needed to make goods to sell, such as factories, raw materials and land) and the proletariat work for the means of production. To be successful, the bourgeoisie must make a profit. They do this by paying the proletariat low wages and making them work long hours.

The proletariat create **surplus value** for the bourgeoisie. For example, it might be the case that in a large supermarket the first four hours of the day are the necessary labour time for the survival of the company. The next four hours are surplus time in which the proletariat create a profit for their employers. Surplus value is created by the surplus unpaid labour of the worker. The proletariat do not know that surplus labour exists; it appears to be paid labour.

Why do the proletariat accept it?

Marx stated that the proletariat are unaware of the exploitation and he referred to this as **false class consciousness**. He referred to the **ideological apparatus of state control** (the agents of socialisation) which are the means of controlling the way the proletariat think; they trick the proletariat into not recognising inequality. The ideological apparatus of state control forms the **superstructure** of society which is designed to support the economy or the **infrastructure**. The law, the family, religion, and education are shaped by the economy to control the proletariat and further the gains of the bourgeoisie. (For an understanding of how education benefits the bourgeoisie, see: Correspondence principle.)

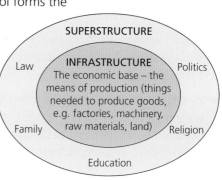

How the family benefits the bourgeoisie

In the diagram, you can see that according to Marxists the family is shaped by the economy for capitalist gains. For example, a man working in a biscuit factory benefits the bourgeoisie in the following ways:

➤ The man's boss (the bourgeoisie) is able to make a profit out of him because he knows that his wife will comfort him after a difficult day at work and do his cooking and cleaning for free, which means that the bourgeoisie can keep workers' wages low.

➤ The family serves the needs of capitalism by reproducing the next generation of workers who will follow their father into the biscuit factory.

➤ When the biscuit company is doing well, the family further benefits the bourgeoisie because the man's wife will work temporarily in the factory as part of a **reserve army of labour**.

➤ The man not only produces the biscuits, but also buys them for his children, thereby increasing the profits of his employer.

How Marxists wanted to change society

Marx and Engels wrote *The Communist Manifesto* to inspire the proletariat to:

➤ make the transition from being a 'class in itself' that was unaware of its exploitation to a 'class for itself' that was class conscious

➤ overthrow the bourgeoisie in a revolution, resulting in a communist state with a shared distribution of wealth achieved by the removal of private property (Marx claimed that 'property is theft').

Marx and Engels believed the existence of the bourgeoisie was becoming incompatible with society and they felt confident that it would be replaced by communism: 'the bourgeoisie produces its own grave diggers. Its fall and the victory of the proletariat are equally inevitable.' (Marx & Engels, 1985)

Neo-Marxism

Neo-Marxists attempted to apply the theory to more recent times ('neo' means new). Two neo-Marxists are included in this book: Harry Braverman, like Marx, was critical of the ways in which craftsmen had become deskilled and alienated from their work; Pierre Bourdieu is considered a neo-Marxist as he recognised the way economic, social and cultural capital combined to give the bourgeoisie more power in society.

Evaluation of Marxism

Strengths	Weaknesses
• It has made a huge contribution to society. It seeks to improve society by reducing inequalities rather than just theorising about them. • It inspired the welfare state which has provided many people with a safety net of benefits and a free National Health Service. • The theory is still relevant today as there is a significant gap between the rich and poor. The recession of 2008 and its aftermath have exposed inequalities in capitalism. • As a macro theory, it connects the individual to the wider society; it recognises structural forces.	• The prediction of a communist revolution has largely not been realised. The majority of the world is capitalist. • It has been criticised for not adequately accounting for the middle classes which have arguably grown in more recent times. • The proletariat might not be falsely class conscious, but prefer the consumer choices and freedoms of capitalism. The proletariat have a vested interest in making a profit for the bourgeoisie (to secure their jobs). • It has been criticised for placing too much focus on the economy – institutions such as education and the family do not exist solely to further the interests of the bourgeoisie.

Think about ...

In what ways might religion control the proletariat for the benefit of the bourgeoisie? (Consider the meaning of Marx's famous quote 'religion is the opium of the people'.)

Reference

MARX, K. & ENGELS, F. (1848) 1985 *The Communist Manifesto*. Introduction by TAYLOR, A. J. P. London: Penguin.

See also: Capital; Correspondence principle; Deskilling; Reserve army of labour; Social class.

Masculinities

Masculinity refers to the characteristics associated with men. Of course, men are not a homogenous group (they are not all the same). Some people would argue therefore that it is perhaps more accurate to write about 'masculinities' rather than 'masculinity'.

A masculine identity is learned during primary socialisation and is reinforced by other agents, including the media and peer group, later in life.

What is masculinity?

Instead of being solely natural, masculine identities are instead nurtured identities. However, the idea that masculinity is something natural persists. For example, in his study of boxing gyms, Chris Matthews found that, although his participants' physiques as boxers did not occur naturally but were the result of many hours of disciplined training, they argued that their behaviour was based on instincts:

❝Chris Matthews: Do you think you learn those traits or are you born with them?

Gary (research participant): It's testosterone and that, ain't it, every man's born wiv' 'em, kid. Who don't want to look after their wife and kids?

Chris: So it's part of being a man?

Gary: That's our job, ain't it, we weren't put on this earth to bake cakes and do washin', was we? You g'back to when we was huntin' and gatherin', it's the men what do all the fightin', ain't it? It's in ya genes youth.❞ (Matthews, 2012)

Hegemonic masculinity

Men tend to be socialised to aspire to a hegemonic or dominant masculinity, characterised by aggression and being physically tough. This is a powerful ideology but one which Raewyn Connell is critical of, arguing that hegemonic masculinities don't reflect the lives of many real men at all. She identified three forms of masculinity in addition to the hegemonic model.

1. **Complicit masculinity:** This is a form of masculinity that supports hegemonic masculinity. It best describes men who would like to be dominant, but recognise that within their peer group they will not be; for example, a man who cheers from the sidelines while his friend is in a fight, or a man who does not objectify his girlfriend, but watches pornographic movies instead.

2. **Marginalised masculinity:** This is a form of masculinity in which some men feel excluded from mainstream masculinity and society itself. Many men have been affected by the loss of British manufacturing and have experienced the feelings of a loss of masculinity as a result.

3. **Subordinated masculinity:** Some men are made to feel inferior for not complying with the hegemonic model – gay men, for example. However, gay men have gained increasing rights, improved status and a greater acceptance in society.

Alpha male to new man (and back again)

The hegemonic model is associated with the concept of the 'alpha male', the idea of a man who is a 'natural' leader, physically tough and seeing himself as superior to women. Yet by the 1980s, the term 'new man' was being used to describe men who were pro-feminism and who pulled their weight at home. Sensitivity was viewed as a desirable characteristic.

The mid-1990s saw the emergence of so-called 'metrosexuals' – young men living city-based consumer lifestyles, interested in fashion and their appearance. The 'new man' and the 'metrosexual' represented a break away from hegemonic masculinity.

However, the mid-1990s also saw the emergence of the 'lad'. In contrast to the 'new man', lad culture was characterised by drinking, fighting and seeing women as sex objects. It was seen as a return to hegemonic masculinity.

Masculinity in crisis?

For many working-class men, a masculine identity could be found in manual work. Over the past 30 years, however, Britain's manufacturing sector has considerably shrunk and most mines have closed down. According to Máirtín Mac an Ghaill, working-class men living in post-industrial towns have experienced a 'crisis of masculinity'. Most jobs are in the service sector, which may not suit ex-manual workers. In addition, girls are outperforming boys across every stage in education and this might add to the sense of crisis. The recession since 2008 has seen many men made redundant and lose their breadwinner role.

There is not just one type of masculinity in society; it is more appropriate to refer to masculinities. There is the possibility of social adaptability; a man might behave like a 'lad' when out drinking with his friends, but take on the role of 'new man' when looking after his children.

Think about ...

Identify examples of characteristics of hegemonic masculinity from the covers of 'lads' magazines. How far do these characteristics apply to men today?

See also:
Femininities;
Patriarchy.

References

CONNELL, R. (1995) *Masculinities.* Cambridge: Polity Press.

MAC AN GHAILL, M. (1994) *The Making of Men: Masculinities, Sexualities and Schooling.* Buckingham: Open University Press.

MATTHEWS, C. R. (2012) *It's testosterone and that – Biology Ideology and the Framing of Manliness.* Loughborough University.

Mass media

In the early years of the twenty-first century, there have been significant changes to the mass media with the rise of digital media sources and of interactive forms of media communication, for example mobile technology. People now have media sources at their fingertips 24/7. The impact the media can have on society is enormous, influencing opinions and behaviours via the portrayal of individuals, groups and actions.

Ownership and control

Ownership of the media

It is apparent that what we define as the media in the twenty-first century is rapidly changing to include the latest developments in technology. However, what all forms of media still entail is 'a process that involves senders, messages and receivers as well as a specific social context in which they operate'. (Briggs & Cobley, 2002)

Media ownership has become concentrated into a few giant media corporations, although this does not mean they hold control of all the messages sent by the media. Around 90 per cent of the biggest companies are American-owned transnational corporations (operating across several countries). As a result of the growing number of transnational corporations, Western consumerism seems to be dominating more and more of the world.

Many companies also become conglomerates, which are companies with cross-media ownership; for example, a company which collectively owns TV channels, radio stations and magazines.

Control of the media

If the situation is that those who own the media also control the content, then they can use this as a means of promoting their own interests. There are two main perspectives on this, as follows.

Marxists believe this can be a way to control the ideology of the masses. As media bosses control who is employed by the company, they therefore control the content, as they will employ people who support their views. Media owners can also have influence on politics; as a result of the power held by the media in society, it could be seen that political parties and leaders want to 'get them onside' in support of their campaigns. Rupert Murdoch of News International was linked with the New Labour campaigns in 1997 and has in the past

controlled the political agenda of *The Sun,* a newspaper widely read by the working classes. For Marxists, this demonstrates an interest in controlling the ideologies of the working class through influence in newspapers targeted primarily at these audiences. (Flowers, 2008)

Neo-Marxists such as Louis Althusser agree that the media aids capitalist ideology, but Althusser does not agree with traditional Marxists that this is purely due to the influence of the owners. It can be argued that media corporations are so complex that it would be impossible for owners to control all views. Althusser believes the media is part of the Ideological State Apparatus, institutions within society which reproduce and legitimate the capitalist ideology. The media contributes to the false consciousness that oppresses the working class; through the media, we are enclosed in a consumer-driven society which values material possessions.

Other perspectives on control

➤ **The functionalist perspective:** With their consensus view of society, functionalists believe that the media supports socialisation and integration into society by communicating shared values, norms and goals to the masses. However, the functionalist perspective can be criticised for being outdated as the mass media are a far more complex entity than this perspective suggests. Also, the notion that audiences are passively absorbing such messages again seems outdated. However, this can also be a criticism of the Marxist perspective.

➤ **The pluralist perspective:** This incorporates ideas of diversity and choice becoming increasingly prominent in society. Thus the media has changed to reflect the rise in ethnic diversity; for example, there are various TV and radio stations aimed specifically at certain groups, such as BBC Asian Network. Jean Blondel (1969, cited in Flowers, 2008) claimed that no single group has monopoly of power and control of the media, and like society, the media is competitive and diverse.

Media effects

Exposure to the mass media can affect the opinions, behaviours and understandings of society that are held by audiences. In a world where digital technology and media sources seem to have an ever-growing influence on members of society, it is increasingly important to attempt to explain their impact. Many sociologists believe we make our own interpretations of the messages we receive from the media, but how we interpret them is greatly influenced by the social context in which we see them.

Sociological explanations for the effects of the media upon audiences vary. Different sociologists have proposed a variety of models to demonstrate the effects of the media; these include models where the audiences are perceived to be active or passive.

Passive model	
Hypodermic model	This is a positivist approach which suggests that the media 'injects' its messages into a passive audience. The audience then reacts to the 'injection' as part of a cause and effect process. For example, there have been cases of criminals accused of 'copycat' crimes and violent attacks based on things they have seen in the media. One of the most famous of these incidents is the two young boys, who murdered two-year-old James Bulger, allegedly using methods based on torture from the film *Child's Play III* which they had just watched.
	A major criticism of this model is from an interactionist perspective, which maintains that audiences are not passive and are therefore not directly influenced by the media. Many young people have watched *Child's Play* and yet are never violent.
Active audience models	
Uses and gratification model	This model suggests that people use the media in various ways to serve different purposes. Dennis McQuail (1972) gives examples of the different uses and gratifications people can gain from the media, such as diversion and identity. Some people use the media as a diversion from everyday life, as a means of escapism. For others, the media confirms their sense of identity as being up-to-date on current affairs or portraying a certain fashionable image.
	Of course the media can have negative effects on some people. For example, the portrayal of skinny models is often blamed for the rise in eating disorders among young people.
Cultural effects model	In this model, David Morley combines elements of the hypodermic and active audience models. From his perspective, the media does have important effects on audiences, but in more of a long-term gradual way than the hypodermic model suggests. Audiences interpret messages in individual ways, but there is a 'dominant' message present which over time impacts on their opinions.
	From a neo-Marxist perspective, the dominant message would be drip-feeding the capitalist ideology into society by promoting wealth.

Media representations

The mass media at times present simplified and stereotypical representations of different social groups. For example, sociologists have been concerned about the portrayal of gender identities and ethnic groups.

Gender representations

Various studies have used **content analysis** methods to investigate the portrayals of women in the media. Diana Meehan (cited in Trowler, 1996) studied American drama serials. Through analysing female characters, she concluded that there were various typologies that women fit into, such as the 'good wife', the 'victim', and the 'decoy' – a woman who appeared a victim or weak but then became the unlikely heroine of the piece. She also found that the women shown as 'bad' often had rebellious and independent characters, whereas the 'good' were domesticated and sensitive. Nicholas Abercrombie (1999) believes that today the media representation of women has changed with many soaps, dramas and comedies starring strong, independent female characters; for example, the women in *Sex and the City*.

Many sociologists interpret these changes as reflecting societal shifts towards increasing gender equality. However, feminists maintain that the women we see on screen still represent stereotyped images, and women's magazines, for example, continue to contain adverts and articles whose sole aim is to achieve 'perfection', which in itself is a media stereotype.

Feminist responses

➤ **Radical feminists** see the media as upholding values of patriarchy and the subservience of women. Anne Ross Muir suggests, 'If a film or television company is a mini sexist society, with women congregated in the lower paid service and support jobs, how can we expect the image of women that they produce to be anything but sexist?' (cited in Trowler, 1996)

➤ **Liberal feminists** argue that the media does produce stereotypical images of women, but progress is being made towards equality. As women are increasingly employed in media organisations, the portrayals should continue to change accordingly. The image of women has changed slowly. Gaye Tuchman suggests that this change is a reflection of a shifting social reality which is also changing at a slow pace.

➤ **Postmodernist** thinkers maintain that the media messages give diversity and choice for gender identities; audiences can interpret the messages in their own ways. They admit that it is true to say the media was sexist in the past, but observe that as public awareness of gender issues grew, particularly through the 1980s, the cultural ideological shift was reflected in the mass media. (Trowler, 1996)

Representations of ethnic groups

TV broadcasting is said to show a restricted range of social roles for minority ethnic groups. In a survey by the Broadcasting Standards Commission in 1999, it was found that:

➤ ethnic minorities featured in 42 per cent of programmes

➤ only 7 per cent of all people with a speaking role were of minority backgrounds

➤ ethnic minority characters were often shown in limited occupational roles which do not accurately represent reality.

As with any media message, the messages about ethnicity can be interpreted in different ways; for example, Sut Jhally and Justin Lewis (1992) studied responses to *The Cosby Show,* a popular US comedy about an upper-middle-class black family. They found that the family were at times seen as positive role models for the black community, but also that they could give an unrepresentative image of black people in the US as the show largely ignores the racism and deprivation faced by many.

Attitudes which could lead to negative perceptions in the wider society have also been found in the subtext of some newspaper articles.

Peter Teo (2000, cited in Bryman, 2012) analysed two Australian newspapers' reports about 5T, a Vietnamese gang involved in drug dealing in Sydney. He found various linguistic techniques were used in the articles to convey certain images of the police force's work to end the problem, but also subversive racism. He noted that the terms 'Asian' and 'Vietnamese' were used so frequently in relation to criminal activity that the two become associated with Australian drug culture.

Think about ...

Watch a few advertisements on TV. Make a list of any gender stereotypes you see. What kinds of images of women are the adverts portraying? How much impact do you think these messages will have on audiences?

See also:
Feminism;
Glass ceiling;
Interpretivism;
Marxism.

References

BRIGGS, A. & COBLEY, P. (2002) *The Media: An Introduction*. Harlow: Pearson Education.

BRYMAN, A. (2012) *Social Research Methods*. 4th Ed. Oxford: Oxford University Press.

FLOWERS, T. (2008) *A2 Sociology*. Cheltenham: Nelson Thornes.

HARALAMBOS, M. & HOLBORN, M. (2000) *Sociology: Themes and Perspectives*. 5th Ed. London: HarperCollins Publishers.

TROWLER, P. (1996) *Investigating Mass Media*. 2nd Ed. London: Collins Educational.

McDonaldization

George Ritzer defined McDonaldization as: 'the process by which the principles of the fast food restaurant are coming to dominate more and more sectors of American society as well as the rest of the world' (Ritzer, 2011). The impact of McDonaldization goes far beyond the fast food industry; its principles and processes have been replicated in the entertainment industry, health care, education, and workplaces and businesses across the world.

Key principles of McDonaldization

The key principles which Ritzer identified are: efficiency, calculability, predictability and control.

Efficiency
This refers to the best way of completing a task quickly and easily. The workers in a McDonaldized industry work efficiently by following step-by-step guidelines rather than using their own creativity.

Calculability
Here the emphasis is on quantity rather than quality and the idea that 'bigger is better'. In a McDonaldized workplace, the quality of the work should not vary as workers are following the same processes, so they will instead be assessed on the quantity of their work: how many burgers can be made in the shortest time? How many customers can be served?

Predictability
This refers to the uniformity and standardisation of a product or service. The consumer expects predictability, which is the appeal of fast food; it is broadly the same across all franchises. The consumer is comforted by the familiarity. In this respect, Ritzer's McDonaldization has been influenced by Fordism, which emphasises the standardisation of mass-produced goods.

Control
Ritzer focused on control through the ways in which humans have been replaced by machines in the workplace

(automation), and also the deskilling of workers. If workers repeat monotonous tasks and do not have to think for themselves, the employer can exercise a greater degree of control over them. Automation also removes the potential for human error and therefore again increases control.

Why has McDonaldization spread?

➤ **Economics:** Lower costs due to efficiency results in greater profits.

➤ **Familiarity:** The golden arches of McDonald's are instantly recognisable and can be seen from afar. Many people can quickly identify a brand from its logo because they have grown up to be familiar with it.

➤ **Lifestyle change:** Fast food and fast service are convenient when both partners in a family are working and leading busy lives. Another lifestyle change which has led to the rise of McDonaldization is the increase in consumerism; as disposable incomes and car ownership have increased, many small local shops have gone out of business as people drive to out-of-town retail parks. (Hannigan, 1998)

Rationality

In *The McDonaldization of Society*, Ritzer drew on the Weberian concept of rationality. By rationality, Max Weber was referring to the idea that individuals are no longer left to their own devices to decide the best way of doing things; instead they have pre-determined rules and procedures to follow. For Weber, rationality came in the form of bureaucracy (the rules and procedures of business administration). For Ritzer, it came in the form of McDonaldization.

'The irrationality of rationality'

Overrationalising a process has the unintended and paradoxical outcome of irrationality, where things do not work as well as intended. Consider, for example, the fact that bureaucracy is often referred to as 'red tape' – the idea that too many rules and forms to fill in slows things down rather than speeding them up. Ritzer points to the following irrationalities of McDonaldization:

➤ **Dehumanisation:** The expectation to follow rigorous rules and procedures takes away the individual's creativity. Lack of choice in society and leading impersonal lives was called the 'iron cage' by Weber. Weber believed that people are encaged or trapped by bureaucracy. Similarly, Ritzer argues that McDonaldization has become an iron cage which is difficult for individuals to escape.

➤ **Damage to the environment:** This is as a result of the mass production of goods and the waste that this tends to entail.

➤ **Damage to health:** Fast food worsens (or arguably leads to) the growing problem of obesity and heart disease in Western countries.

➤ **Inefficiency:** The popularity of fast food can create inefficiency and 'slow food' as people sit waiting for a long time in a drive through.

Think about ...

Visit a local shopping centre. What examples of the McDonaldization process can you identify?

References

See also:
Consumer culture;
Disneyization;
Fordism.

HANNIGAN, J. (1998) *Fantasy City: Pleasure and Profit in the Postmodern Metropolis*. London: Routledge.

RITZER, G. (2011) *The McDonaldization of Society*. London: Sage Publications.

Meritocracy

Meritocracy is the system of rewards in exchange for hard work and ability. Such rewards include academic qualifications, money and medals for sporting achievements. A society can be described as meritocratic if people achieve their status through merit rather than acquiring it through background. Functionalists believe that a meritocratic system is fair. Marxists, however, argue that meritocracy is a myth and that society is neither equal nor fair.

Meritocracy: a fair system?

A meritocratic system requires competition. Competition, in theory, enables the best people to be selected for each position. Consider a typical job application process. Some candidates' applications will be rejected because their qualifications are not as high or their previous experience is not as relevant as that of other candidates. The candidates who are selected for interview will usually be interviewed by the same interview panel, asked the same questions and required to complete the same tasks as each other. This means that a fair selection process can be carried out. It is assumed to be meritocratic because the candidates appear to have had equal opportunities.

According to Peter Saunders, while society is unequal, it is not necessarily unfair. He argues that ability and ambition are what matters and that if individuals are talented and work hard, they will be rewarded. Saunders further argues that the giving of unequal rewards for different positions has the positive impact of motivating people to work harder (Saunders, 1990). However, in the example of the job interview, a candidate is not always selected on a meritocratic basis. The interviewer might perhaps know the candidate through an 'old boys' network' and offer the position based on who they know rather than what they know. The chosen candidate might have valuable work experience from an internship that their wealthy and well-connected parents arranged for them. Now the seemingly fair system of selection might not be so meritocratic after all.

Meritocracy and education

According to the functionalist Talcott Parsons, the education system is meritocratic, rewarding students fairly on their effort and ability. Parsons said that meritocracy was vital for **role allocation**. This is the process by which people are slotted into the roles which best suit their abilities in society. Society needs role allocation in order to function because not everyone can be a doctor; all roles need to be fulfilled for the smooth running of society. Meritocracy thereby legitimises different levels of reward according to academic abilities. For functionalists, education is meritocratic and students have equal chances to succeed because:

➤ students in the same class have been taught by the same teacher

➤ students learn the same curriculum (especially true since the introduction of a national curriculum in 1988) and therefore have equal opportunities to succeed

➤ students sit the same national exams.

Myth of meritocracy

Marxists take a different view of education and the wider society; they argue that we have been sold a myth of meritocracy as a means of legitimising inequality and making it seem fair. Samuel Bowles and Herbert Gintis claim that rewards in society are allocated on the basis of class background rather than on ability. The significant social class gap in GCSE results is evidence to support Bowles and Gintis's claim. If education was a meritocracy, we would expect to see the best and worst results from students of all class backgrounds. What we see instead is a marked social class difference. In 2009, approximately one in five of the poorest fifth of students achieved five or more GCSEs at grades A*–C including English and maths, compared to nearly three-quarters of the richest fifth (this is a considerable gap of over 50 percentage points). (Chowdry et al, 2009)

'Birth not worth'

Alan Milburn was appointed by the government to review social mobility in the UK and he stated that 'birth not worth' is the deciding factor in the course an individual's life will take (Milburn, 2012). This means that the social class background a child is born into seems to have a bigger impact than the child's individual efforts. Despite some efforts to open up professional occupations to people from a range of backgrounds, such occupations remain very elitist; for example, while only 7 per cent of the population is educated privately, 15 out of the 17 Supreme Court judges went to private school.

Think about ...

Identify an example where people in society:

a) are not rewarded for their hard work and ability

b) are rewarded despite a lack of hard work and ability.

See also:
Functionalism;
Marxism; Status.

References

BOWLES, S. & GINTIS, H. (1976) *Schooling in Capitalist America*. London: Routledge.

CHOWDRY, H., CRAWFORD, C. & GOODMAN, A. (2009) *Drivers and Barriers to Educational Success: Evidence from the Longitudinal Study of Young People in England*. Institute for Fiscal Studies. Department for Children, Schools and Families. [Online] Available from: http://discovery.ucl.ac.uk/18314/1/18314.pdf. [Accessed: 23rd February 2013].

MILBURN, A. (2012) *Fair Access to Professional Careers: A Progress report by the Independent Reviewer on Social Mobility and Child Poverty*. [Online] Available from: https://www.gov.uk/government/uploads/system/uploads/attachment_data/file/61090/IR_FairAccess_acc2. [Accessed: 23rd February 2013].

SAUNDERS, P. (1990) *Social Class and Stratification*. London: Routledge.

Moral panic

'Moral panic' is a term used to describe the process by which an event or group of people in society causes the public to feel a sense of threat. The media reporting of the issue creates an exaggeration of the significance of the event to the point where concern about the event grows and causes widespread panic.

Youth 'delinquency' and moral panics

In the 1960s, Stanley Cohen was interested in the media coverage and reaction to the disturbances between two youth subcultures of the time, the Mods and Rockers. Mods and Rockers entered the public consciousness following the reporting of disturbances created by the two groups on the beach in Clacton on a bank holiday in 1964.

Cohen talked to the Mods and Rockers about what happened and then saw an entirely different version of events in the newspapers the following day. The young people involved said that the disturbances were mostly due to boredom; small seaside towns largely catered for families and young children. Cohen, however, noted that the fights were exaggerated by the press. The papers used phrases such as an 'orgy of destruction' and described the disturbances as 'battles'. A Brighton paper stated that on the bank holiday, the beach was deserted due to fear of the teenage mobs. In reality the beach was quiet due to bad weather. (Cohen, 1972)

The media response triggered an overreaction and police presence was stepped up to reassure the public. This then added to the problem as it caused more young people to arrive. The Mods and Rockers had become 'folk devils', blamed for problems in society. The message given was that the beach was for families and young children, that groups of teenagers were not welcome.

The sequence of events causing a moral panic creates a cycle as shown in the diagram:

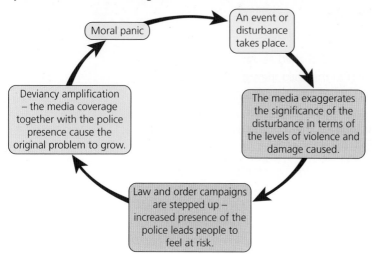

Examples of contemporary moral panics

Asian British men in relation to violence and religion

Since 9/11, there has been a rise in Islamophobia and the vilification of young Asian men by the media. According to Rayen Salgado-Pottier, they have become the centre of a moral panic and are today's folk devils, subject to stereotypes about terrorism. Citing a study by *The Guardian*, Salgado-Pottier noted that in some newspapers the word 'Islamic' was often juxtaposed with the words 'extremist' and 'fundamentalism' which, intended or otherwise, had the effect of making the reader anxious about Islam.

Salagado-Pottier interviewed young people (predominantly Bangladeshi males) in a youth club in Tower Hamlets in London's East End. She found that because of an increased sense of prejudice and discrimination, the young people she interviewed were keen to strengthen their Muslim identity.

Salagado-Pottier argued that this could benefit the young people's lives and their communities, but that it could also lead to deviancy amplification as hostility from the wider society could make some young Muslim men more vulnerable to extremism.

Paedophilia

Although in most cases of child abuse, the abuser is someone known to the child, newspapers give an impression that children are at a constant risk of 'stranger danger'. Many parents grew up when public safety announcements warned them of the risk from strangers and this may have heightened their sense of fear.

In the year 2000, a campaign by a tabloid newspaper of 'naming and shaming' suspected paedophiles caused violent vigilante action (when people try to take the law into their own hands) and widespread panic but did not necessarily make children safer. Chas Critcher stated that 'Moral panics distort our capacity for understanding, even when they appear to recognise a genuine problem.' (Critcher, 2003)

Think about ...

Read the following quote from Cohen and identify ways in which 'chavs' have become the folk devils of today.

'Our society as present structured will continue to generate problems for some of its members – like working-class adolescents – and then condemn whatever solution these groups find.' (Cohen, 1972)

See also: 'Dark side' of family life; Deviance; Subculture.

References

COHEN, S. (1972) *Folk Devils and Moral Panics: The Creation of Mods and Rockers*. London: MacGibbon and Kee.

CRITCHER, C. (2003) *Moral Panics and the Media*. Milton Keynes: Open University Press.

SALGADO-POTTIER, R. (2008) A Modern Moral Panic: The Representation of British Bangladeshi and Pakistani Youth in Relation to Violence and Religion. *Anthropology Matters Journal*. 10 (1).

Multiculturalism

Multiculturalism refers to the coexistence of different ethnic groups in society. In a multicultural society, the government states that all ethnic groups should have equal rights and are entitled to practise their own culture and to form communities. It is similar to cultural diversity and the two terms are often used interchangeably. Cultural diversity means differences in the norms and values between groups. Multiculturalism refers to different ethnic groups living side by side in society.

Mass immigration in the UK

Following the Second World War, there were labour shortages in Britain. The government decided to address this by inviting people from Commonwealth countries to move to Britain to work. In 1948, a ship called the Empire Windrush brought 492 Caribbean men to Britain for work. While black people had lived in Britain for centuries, the Windrush was symbolic because it marked the beginnings of mass immigration. (Fryer, 1999)

In the early years of mass immigration, assimilation was the favoured policy; it stated that minority ethnic groups should lose their old norms and values and adopt the way of life of the 'host' community. However, by the late 1960s, this practice was replaced by multiculturalism. Different ethnic groups set up their own communities with their own businesses, selling food and clothing in keeping with their culture. Such communities also set up their own places of worship and in some cases faith schools.

Multiculturalism and Census data

The UK in its entirety is not multicultural; rural areas, for example, are less diverse than inner city areas. However, it is clear from Census data that British society has become more multicultural; for example, in 2001, nearly 87 per cent of people stated that their ethnic group was White British compared to 80.5 per cent in 2011. In London, the White British group went from being the majority of the city's population in 2001 (approximately 60 per cent) to the minority in 2011 (approximately 45 per cent).

Many of the UK's cities are very multicultural with different ethnic groups living in separate communities. Birmingham is a good example: the 2011 Census reveals that over 86 per cent of the residents of Sutton Coldfield in the north of Birmingham are White British and less than 1 per cent is Pakistani. However, in Washwood Heath, an area near the city centre, just under 10 per cent of the population are White British and 57 per cent are Pakistani. (ONS, 2011)

'Rivers of Blood'

In 1968, the Conservative MP Enoch Powell delivered one of the most controversial speeches in recent British history. The speech was named 'Rivers of Blood'. Powell predicted that multiculturalism would cause violence between groups. He said: 'As I look ahead, I am filled with foreboding. Like the Roman, I seem to see the River Tiber foaming with much blood' (cited in Hewitt, 2005). He gave the speech in reaction to a proposed Race Relations Bill which would make discrimination against ethnic minority groups illegal. He believed that the legislation would harm white British people and said that it was like 'watching a nation busily engaged in heaping up its own funeral pyre'. Powell's speech divided opinion. There was a growing anti-racist movement in the UK and Powell was sacked following his controversial speech. The bill went ahead, but Powell's sacking caused a backlash from many of the white working-class population who wanted him reinstated. Powell had treated minority ethnic groups as a scapegoat on which people could put blame for a lack of housing and jobs.

There was indeed violence as Powell had predicted. For example, there were riots in Brixton in 1981 and Bradford in 2001; and in 2005, 52 people were killed in the 7/7 bombings in London which were carried out by British-born terrorists. More recently, there were riots in 2011 which began in Tottenham. However, there is disagreement about whether this was due to a lack of shared values, or due to poverty and the marginalisation of minority ethnic groups in the UK.

Multiculturalism today

In 2011, the Prime Minister, David Cameron, argued that multiculturalism had failed, causing different groups to lead separate lives. However, according to Paul Gilroy, new types of ethnic identities are developing and cultures are mixing together. He argued that the identities of black people in Britain are influenced by both the culture of the Caribbean and British culture (Gilroy, 1993). His thinking is in line with the ideas that, for young people in particular, identities are becoming more hybrid or mixed rather than separate cultures living side by side.

Think about ...

Enter your postcode in the Office for National Statistics (ONS) website (http://neighbourhood.statistics.gov.uk). Look at the data on ethnicity. Would you describe the area you live in as multicultural?

See also: Culture; Hybridity; Institutional racism.

References

FRYER, P. (1999) *The Politics of the Windrush*. Coventry: Index Books.

GILROY, P. (1993) *The Black Atlantic: Modernity and Double Consciousness*. London: Verso.

HEWITT, R. (2005) *White Backlash and the Politics of Multiculturalism*. Cambridge: Cambridge University Press

OFFICE FOR NATIONAL STATISTICS (2011) Full data set view 2001 and 2011. [Online] Available from: http://neighbourhood.statistics.gov.uk. [Accessed: 3rd March 2013].

Nature versus nurture

The extent to which behaviour is influenced by genetics as opposed to the environment is a long-standing debate. The phrase 'nature versus nurture' was coined in the 1800s by Francis Galton (cousin of Charles Darwin), and since then the debate has generated much scientific research. The debate is about how far an individual is like their parents because of shared DNA, or how far it is due to being raised by them.

Nature, nurture or both?

Characteristics mostly caused by genetics	Characteristics caused by the environment
Eye colour; natural hair colour; skin colour; genetic diseases, such as cystic fibrosis and sickle cell anaemia.	Language; accents; fashion; taste in music; favourite sports; favourite foods.

Characteristics caused by both genetics and environment
Intelligence: Hans Eysenck (1971) controversially claimed that genes determine a student's success in education. However, this has been disputed as there is a considerable gap in the GCSE results of working-class and middle-class students. It is also difficult to produce a culture-free test to measure 'innate' intelligence. The questions on IQ tests might favour the middle classes and their families might be better equipped to support the student taking the test.
Physique: Most men naturally have more muscle mass than most women. However, both men and women can significantly change their physique by weightlifting and bodybuilding; this is therefore cultural rather than natural.
Aggression: There is a link between the hormone testosterone and levels of aggression. Freud claimed that aggression was instinctive. However, it could be due to socialisation; for example, the social expectation that boys' fight could be learned from older brothers, a violent peer group, or the mass media.

Arguments for nature

Studies of twins are used to illustrate the influence of genes. There are cases of identical twins who have grown up apart and yet have similar interests and behaviours. If it was the environment alone that influenced behaviour, such twins, while looking the same, would have very different characters. Research by Archontaki et al (2012) of more than 800 sets of twins revealed that identical twins were twice as likely to share the same personality traits as twins who were not identical. This shows the influence of DNA because identical twins have the same genetic make-up.

Arguments for nurture

John Locke used the term 'tabula rasa' ('blank slate') to claim that behaviour is due to the environment. If babies are born as a blank slate this suggests it is the influence of others in society which forms imprints on their characters.

Research by Margaret Mead supports the idea that behaviour is determined by the environment. She studied three tribes in New Guinea and found considerable variation in gender roles. Traditionally, males in Western society have been associated with dominance and women with passivity, but in one of the tribes Mead studied (the Tchambuli), the men gossiped and decorated themselves while the women were more assertive and practical. If gender roles were natural, there would not be significant variations between cultures. (Mead, 1942)

A number of cases of children who have experienced severe neglect, often referred to as 'feral children', have shown the importance of nurture. The most documented case is Genie, who was locked in her bedroom for the first 13 years of her life, spending her days strapped to a potty chair and her nights strapped to a cot, with almost no human interaction. When she was rescued from her father she could not talk or walk. She had not had primary socialisation. Over the years, Genie made a lot of progress with a team of psychologists and scientists, but while she had learned many words, she could not easily string a sentence together. She had missed the critical period for acquiring language (around five years old). Genie showed the importance of nurture in human development. (Rymer, 1994)

Co-dependence of nature and nurture

While nurture is the key interest of sociologists, in most cases it is the interaction of nature and nurture which explains behaviour. The idea of a blank slate has been rejected by many, but so too have explanations for behaviour based solely on genetics.

Researchers from King's College London found in a study of twins that the extent to which environment influenced behaviour depended on where the children grew up. For example, in London the environment played a greater role than it did in other areas – possibly because of the huge variation in wealth within even the same area of the city, which might mean that twins could meet very different groups of friends who could influence their behaviour than might be the case in a small village. (Davis, 2012)

Think about ...

Think of a talent or behaviour you share with a parent or sibling. Do you think you have this in common because of similar genes, or is it due to shared experiences and imitation or copying?

See also: Agency and structure; Culture; Socialisation.

References

ARCHONTAKI, D., LEWIS, G. J. & BATES, T. C. (2012) Genetic Influences on Psychological Well-Being: A Nationally Representative Twin Study. *Journal of Personality*. Wiley Periodicals.

EYSENCK, H. J. (1971) *Race, Intelligence and Education*. London: Temple Smith.

MEAD, M. (1942) *Growing up in New Guinea: A Study of Adolescence and Sex in Primitive Societies*. Harmondsworth: Penguin.

RYMER, R. (1994) *Genie: A Scientific Tragedy*. New York: HarperPerennial.

WELLCOME TRUST (2012) Nature or nurture? It may depend on where you live. 12th June. [Online] Available from: http://www.wellcome.ac.uk/News/Media-office/Press-releases/2012/WTVM055447.htm. [Accessed: 26th January 2013].

NEETs

NEET is an acronym used by the British government for 16–24-year-olds who are Not in Education, Employment or Training. In November 2012, nearly one in five (17 per cent) of 16–24-year-olds were NEETs, accounting for approximately one million young people. If previous trends continue, roughly half of these young people will still be NEETs one year on. (Britton, 2011)

Examples of NEETs

NEETS are a diverse group. Examples may include:

➤ 16-year-olds who left school at the end of Year 11 with few or no qualifications

➤ 17-year-olds who began A levels or other level 3 courses, but then dropped out before completing

➤ 18-year-olds who completed their A levels, but failed to secure a place at university and are looking for work.

Although NEETs might be associated with 'drop outs', the reality is that many young people find themselves in this situation so it cannot be attributed to the behaviour of individuals alone.

Possible causes of NEETs

➤ A curriculum that focuses too much on assessment targets, and not enough on vocational (work-based) training. Many young people therefore lack the skills needed by employers. Many NEETs have difficulty with literacy and numeracy skills. (Britton, 2011)

➤ Increased costs of education. In 2010, the Education Maintenance Allowance was scrapped. The EMA gave 16–19-year-old students with a household income of less than £33,950 up to £30 per week to support them with further education. In 2011, tuition fees for many universities tripled to over £9,000. These costs may put some young people off studying for fear of debt.

➤ Competition with increasing numbers of graduates for jobs.

➤ A lack of jobs available following a recession. However, Jack Britton observes that the 2008 recession had a limited impact on the number of NEETs. (Britton, 2011)

Strategies to prevent NEEThood

Not only does being NEET have a detrimental impact on future life chances, but NEETs also negatively affect the economy. In 2011, the total cost of NEETs in the UK was over £18 billion (Rogers, 2012). The government has introduced many strategies to reduce the number of NEETs, but it could be argued that cuts to education in the early years of the twenty-first century will increase the problem.

Party in power	Strategy to reduce the number of NEETs
Conservative Party, 1979–1997. The New Right government led by Margaret Thatcher, succeeded by John Major.	**New vocationalism** – following the increase in youth unemployment in the 1970s, the government wanted the education system to be responsible for equipping young people with the skills needed by the workplace. This involved a number of new schemes, including: **Youth Training Scheme (YTS)** – introduced in the early 1980s. A one-year training scheme for young people after leaving school. It was replaced by Youth Training (YT) which included formal qualifications in addition to training.
Labour Party, 1997–2010. The New Labour government led by Tony Blair, succeeded by Gordon Brown.	**New Deal for Young People** – aimed at 18–24-year-olds who had been unemployed for six months or more. This provided young people with a personal advisor to assist with finding education and training opportunities. **Education Maintenance Allowances (EMA)** – introduced nationwide in 2004, EMA was abolished by the coalition government in 2010.

Conservative Liberal Democratic coalition government led by David Cameron, 2010 to the present day.	**Raising the participation age (RPA)** – proposed by the previous Labour government and being realised by the coalition government from 2013. Young people will continue in education or training to the end of the academic year in which they turn 17. (Department for Education, 2012) **Youth Contract** – designed to help 16–17-year-olds to move into education, training or employment with training. Employers will be paid for securing employment with young people. The programme is for those with one or no GCSEs graded A*–C, young offenders who have been released from custody and young people who have been, or are still, in care. (Department for Education, 2013)

Think about ...

What do you consider to be the most important factor in preventing young people from becoming NEET?

See also: Life chances; Poverty; Social mobility.

References

BRITTON, J. (2011) *The Early Bird: Preventing Young People from Becoming a NEET Statistic*. Department of Economics and CMPO, University Of Bristol. [Online] Available from: http://www.nccesb.org.uk/pdfs/Publications/January%202012/publications-bristol-uni-the-early-bird-neet-report-november%202011.pdf. [Accessed: 10th February 2013].

DEPARTMENT FOR EDUCATION (2012) Raising the participation age. [Online] Available from: http://www.education.gov.uk/vocabularies/educationtermsandtags/6877. [Accessed: 10th February 2013].

DEPARTMENT FOR EDUCATION (2013) Youth Contract provision for 16- and 17-year-olds not in education, employment or training. [Online] Available from: http://www.education.gov.uk/childrenandyoungpeople/youngpeople/participation/a00203664/youth-contract. [Accessed: 10th February 2013].

ROGERS, S. (2012) Not in Education, Employment or Training: Europe's Lost NEET Generation Detailed. *The Guardian*. [Online] Available from: http://www.guardian.co.uk/news/datablog/2012/oct/22/not-in-education-employment-training-europe-neet. [Accessed: 10th February 2013].

New Age Movements

The term 'New Age Movements' refers to a group of Western spiritual practices that developed in the second half of the twentieth century and have been especially popular in the early years of the twenty-first century. The trend is sometimes linked to the 'Harry Potter generation' and a renewed interest in magic and other such phenomena.

Features of New Age Movements

New Age Movements (NAMs) do not necessarily seem 'religious' on the surface; they tend to be practices which incorporate themes of nature, astrology or other spiritual elements. Examples of NAMs include: tarot, feng shui, reflexology, crystal healing and astrology.

Unlike mainstream religious practices, NAMs do not usually have any central organisation or formal membership. Participants can 'dip in and out' of the practices freely. Postmodernists describe this as 'pick and mix' religion. It is a feature of a diverse and pluralist society, where people are able to sample different spiritualities until they find one that suits their lifestyle and spiritual needs.

Types of NAMs

Rodney Stark and William Sims Bainbridge (cited in Webb et al, 2009) broadly categorise NAMs (cults) into two main types:

1. **Audience cults:** These lack any central organisation and do not have any formal membership. They often require little or no commitment and participants will not usually interact with each other; they could even participate via the media. Example: astrology.

2. **Client cults:** These are based on the relationship between a consultant and their client; for example,

people who offer alternative therapies and treatments. Examples: spiritualism, reflexology.

Paul Heelas (cited in Webb et al, 2009) estimated that around 146,000 people are participating in 2,000 different New Age activities in the UK.

What is the appeal of the New Age?

➤ A spiritual void might be filled without the need for traditional religion, or people might be disillusioned with the mainstream.

➤ People want something more from their life; with the New Age, personal experiences are valued, so people do not need to look to external sources such as scripture for validation.

➤ The New Age statistically has more women members. This trend is possibly explained through the focus on 'the natural' which seems to appeal more to female characteristics.

Think about ...

Research the key ideas and beliefs of reflexology and find out if it is available in your local area. Why do you think this treatment would appeal to different local people?

See also: NRMs.

References

BRUCE, S. (1996) Religion in Britain at the Close of the 20th Century: A Challenge to the Silver Lining Perspective. *Journal of Contemporary Religion*. 11 (3). p.273.

HARALAMBOS, M. & HOLBORN, M. (2000) *Sociology: Themes and Perspectives*. 5th Ed. London: HarperCollins Publishers.

WEBB, R., WESTERGAARD, H., TROBE, K. & STEEL, L. (2009) *A2 Sociology*. Brentwood: Napier Press.

Norms

Norms are rules or guidelines that define what is seen as appropriate behaviour in society. Norms may be written; for example, school rules and the Ten Commandments. However, they are often unwritten, everyday expectations of behaviour; for example, saying 'please' and 'thank you' when paying in a shop. Norms are seen as automatic, taken-for-granted actions, but they are in fact *learned* during primary and secondary socialisation.

Relationship between norms and values

Note this key difference between norms and values: norms are specific actions; values are general beliefs.

Agent of socialisation	Examples of norms	The values behind the norms
The family	Parent giving child a kiss before school	Love and affection
Peer group	Teenager buying a certain brand of trainers to 'fit in'	Conformity and belonging

Culturally-specific norms

Norms vary between societies. For example, in France it is customary to kiss someone on both cheeks when greeting. In the UK it is the norm to say 'hello' or maybe just kiss once.

In most Western societies, making eye contact is a social norm when talking to someone. It shows you are listening. However, in some parts of Africa and Asia, the norm is to lower the eyes when someone considered higher in status is talking. Many young people do this when an older adult is talking to them, as a mark of respect.

The norms of Amish culture

The Amish are a religious group mostly living in communities in North America and known for their simple way of life with very little use of modern technology.

Amish norms are known as the **Ordnung**. This sets out rules for Amish people based on scripture. The norms vary between Amish communities and are voted on each year by members of the specific community. They include:

➤ Plain and simple clothing, with long dresses for women.

➤ Farming – they are largely self-sufficient and believe that working the land brings them closer to God.

➤ Rumspringa (to 'roam around') – this is a time for young adults to explore the outside world. It might include drinking alcohol, dating, having a job and wearing any clothes they choose. The idea is that they will then make an informed decision about whether to be baptised into the church.

➤ Shunning – an individual who leaves the church after joining is normally shunned. Leaving carries a huge social stigma.

Breaking norms

Breaking norms is seen as deviance. Most norms are not set out in law so breaking them is not criminal, but there are sanctions to prevent the breaching of norms to ensure solidarity in society; for example, a woman wearing a white dress to a friend's wedding in Western culture would normally be breaking a norm by 'upstaging the bride'. The sanction might be unpopularity.

Think about ...

Identify five examples of religious norms.

Reference

See also: Culture; Socialisation; Subculture; Values.

Exploring Amish Country. [Online] Available from: http://www.exploring-amish-country.com/amish-culture.html. [Accessed: 17th January 2013].

NRMs

New Religious Movements (NRMs) are alternative spiritual movements that have grown since the 1960s. They grew out of the 'hippie' culture and rebellion against dominant social norms and the mainstream church. Interest in Eastern spirituality increased around this time, leading to a growth in new spiritual movements which incorporated aspects of Eastern faiths, Christianity and Western psychotherapies. Some NRMs fuse these themes; others are more like 'self-help' ideas than 'religions', focusing on individuals' success and fulfilment.

Types of NRMs

Roy Wallis classified three main types of NRMs:

➤ **World rejecting:** These movements are sect-like in character, demand high levels of commitment from members and claim sole knowledge of the truth. They often have a 'charismatic leader'. Examples: International Society for Krishna Consciousness (Hare Krishna), People's Temple.

➤ **World accommodating:** These often incorporate aspects of mainstream religion, but give them renewed vitality by moving away from the restrictions of traditional doctrine. They also have a greater focus on spirituality, for example personal experiences of God. They are not against the world, and members can continue with their usual life but will generally give a proportion of time to the movement and spiritual practices. Examples: Raelian Movement, Charismatic and Pentecostal churches.

➤ **World affirming:** These movements are concerned mainly with 'unlocking human potential' and self-realisation. Often they can appear non-religious with a focus on the individual rather than the divine. They tend to require lower levels of commitment from members, and can be rather informal. Example: Transcendental Meditation. (Aldridge, 2007)

Why do NRMs appeal?

Max Weber claimed that NRMs often appeal to people who feel marginalised in society as they offer stability and a sense of community. This might be particularly appropriate for world-rejecting movements as they tend to be small, close-knit communities. Reasons for marginalisation might include poverty or 'relative deprivation' in middle-class groups (those who are spiritually deprived or feel caught up in materialistic, consumerist life).

Bryan Wilson believes that NRMs emerge in times of social change, for example war and economic or political change. These ideas could be a useful link to Marxist theory of religion. Karl Marx claimed that religion is the 'opium of the people'; it could be argued that Weber and Wilson's ideas support this because they are saying that NRMs only attract people who are in situations of insecurity and so need some sort of comfort and hope.

Think about ...

1. Watch the BBC's *Panorama – Scientology and Me* on YouTube. Explain why the media often portrays NRMs negatively and why their use of the word 'cult' is often inaccurate.

2. Explain why NRMs have a high turnover of members.

See also:
Marxism; New Age Movements; Weberianism.

References

ALDRIDGE, A. (2007) *Religion in the Contemporary World*. Cambridge: Polity Press.

PARTRIDGE, C. & MELTON, G. (2004) *Encyclopedia of New Religions*. Oxford: Lion Hudson.

WALLIS, R. (1984) *Elementary Forms of the New Religious Life*. London: Routledge and Kegan Paul.

Organic analogy

In structural functionalist theory, an organic analogy is used to compare society to the human body. Just as the body is made up of different organs that contribute to the overall health of the body, so society is made up of different institutions (such as family, education, the mass media) that must work together to ensure the smooth running of society. If one part of the body or society has problems, it can cause disorder elsewhere.

The work of Herbert Spencer

According to Spencer (cited in Bhatt, 2011), the body and society are alike in the following ways:

➤ The body and society both grow over time; a baby becomes an adult; some small villages grow into cities.

➤ As both grow, their structures become more complex.

➤ Both the body and society consist of the following three systems:

1. **The sustaining system:** Just as the body needs sustenance or nourishment to survive, so too does society need support.

2. **The circulatory system:** In the body, the circulatory system transports blood around the body so that organs can work efficiently; in society, the road and railway networks, together with forms of communication, including the internet, keep society operating.

3. **The regulatory system:** In the body, this is known as the central nervous system; in society, it is the role of the government from which all other institutions obtain their rules.

➤ Both the body and society adapt to changes in the environment.

➤ In both the body and society, there is an interdependence of its parts.

Criticisms

➤ Society is unlike the human body because the body follows a lifecycle from birth to death. Societies, on the other hand, do not die but adapt to changes and continue to evolve.

➤ Unlike the people who make up the institutions of society, the organs in the body have no choice but to work together.

➤ Robert Merton criticised the idea of unity and solidarity in society. Somewhat unusually for a functionalist, he argued that society was characterised by conflict. (Merton, 1957)

Think about ...

Explain how problems in the education system might cause dysfunction in other areas of society.

See also:
Functionalism.

References

BHATT, A. (2011) Complete information on Herbert Spencer's Organic Analogy. Preserve Articles. [Online] Available from: http://www.preservearticles.com/201101173445/complete-information-on-herbert-spencers-organic-analogy.html. [Accessed: 4th January 2013].

MERTON, R. (1957) *Social Theory and Social Structure*. New York: Free Press of Glencoe.

Patriarchy

The literal meaning of patriarchy is 'rule of fathers'. It is a term used for male dominance. Despite the rise of feminism and a move towards equality, the majority of the world can still be described as patriarchal. In the UK, in most institutions, power is held in the hands of men.

Patriarchy in the workplace

Patriarchy in the workplace can best be explained with reference to the 'glass ceiling'. Women also experience disadvantage in terms of pay. The Fawcett Society, which campaigns for gender equality, states that, although it is now over forty years since the 1970 Equal Pay Act, on average for every £100 men earn, women earn £85 (Fawcett Society, 2010). Research by the Chartered Management Institute (CMI, 2010) suggests that equal pay is not likely until 2067.

Patriarchy in the family

Examples of patriarchy in the family include women doing the majority of the cooking and cleaning for men, and deferring to their husbands in decision making. An extreme but not uncommon form of patriarchy is domestic violence.

Many housewives experience boredom and frustration with the monotony of housework. In *The Feminine Mystique*, Betty Friedan wrote about women's dissatisfaction with family life. Her book became a best-seller because it spoke to and for many women and lifted the lid on women's unhappiness at being subordinated to men. Friedan referred to the 'problem that had no name'. (Friedan, 1963)

In 2012, analysis by the Institute for Public Policy Research think tank shows that just one in ten married men does the same amount of cleaning and washing as his wife. (Darlington, 2012)

Patriarchy in the mass media

Patriarchy in the mass media includes portrayals of women in narrow and subordinated roles as a housewife, a mother or a sex object. In 1990, Guy Cumberbatch studied 500 television advertisements and found that men were twice as likely to be shown in paid employment, with 89 per cent of adverts using a male voice-over.

In more recent years, the representation of women in the media has improved. David Gauntlett carried out a content analysis of television programmes and found 'female and male characters are likely to be as intelligent – or stupid – as each other'. (Gauntlett, 2002)

However, ownership of the media is still overwhelmingly male. All of the major national tabloid and broadsheet newspapers in the UK are owned by men. Perhaps one of the clearest signs of patriarchy in the media is that the most famous feature of the most widely read newspaper in the UK is a picture of a topless woman!

Patriarchy in politics

Women are underrepresented in politics which leads to concerns that the needs and interests of women will also be underrepresented in the wider society. The chief executive of the Fawcett Society, Ceri Goddard, considers the lack of representation of women to be a blow to democracy. She states 'if we're not at the table, we're on the menu'. In 2012:

➤ men outnumbered women by four to one in the UK Parliament

➤ of 23 cabinet members, only four were women. (Fawcett Society, 2012)

The end of men?

According to Hanna Rosin, women are now overtaking men at home and in the workplace. In her controversial book, *The End of Men and the Rise of Women*, she argues that the balance now tips in favour of women and that recession has been particularly difficult for men (Rosin, 2012). However, although there has been a trend towards gender equality, the evidence that society is patriarchal is overwhelming.

Think about ...

With reference to the representation of women in politics, what do you understand by the quote 'if we're not at the table, we're on the menu'?

See also: 'Dark side' of family life; Glass ceiling.

References

CMI (2010) Equal Pay still 57 years away. [Online] Available from: http://www.managers.org.uk/practical-support/management-community/professional-networks/equal-pay-still-57-years-away/. [Accessed: 2nd December 2012].

DARLINGTON, R. (2012) Real men do housework. 12th March. [Online] Available from: http://www.ippr.org/articles/56/8837/real-men-do-housework/. [Accessed: 2nd December 2012].

FAWCETT SOCIETY (2010) Equal Pay. [Online] Available from: http://www.fawcettsociety.org.uk/index.asp?PageID=23/. [Accessed: 2nd December 2012].

FAWCETT SOCIETY (2012) If we're not at the table, we're on the menu. [Online] Available from: http://www.fawcettsociety.org.uk/documents/Women%20in%20Power-%20Facts%20and%20Stats%20August%20 2012/. [Accessed: 2nd December 2012].

FRIEDAN, B. (1963) *The Feminine Mystique*. New York: Dell.

GAUNTLETT, D. (2002) *Media, Gender and Identity*. London: Routledge. Cited in Haralambos et al (2004) *Sociology in Focus for OCR AS Level*. Lancashire: Causeway Press.

ROSIN, H. (2012) *The End of Men and the Rise of Women*. New York: Viking.

Positivism

Positivism is a branch of Sociology which claims that society can be studied scientifically, that we can apply principles of objectivity and detachment from the natural sciences to social research. Positivists are interested in identifying patterns in human behaviour. They are macro-level sociologists who look for structural explanations of society.

Positivism includes the following general principles:

➤ The role of theory is to generate a hypothesis (prediction) which can be tested.

➤ The identification of cause and effect forms the basis of universal laws. Such laws are described as social facts.

➤ Research must remain objective.

Scientific research is based on logic and clear methodology. A scientist will observe patterns in nature and develop laws of cause and effect to explain them. For positivists, social research should aim to observe and explain patterns found in human behaviour. (Webb et al, 2009)

Durkheim on suicide

Emile Durkheim maintained that social facts cause our behaviours, and as a **structuralist** sociologist he saw these behaviours as governed by the innate structure of society. He believed the suicide rate was a social fact. He used quantitative data from official statistics to analyse the suicide rates for various European countries. This enabled him to establish theories about the suicide patterns among different social groups. He concluded that these were the result of social forces acting on individuals.

Falsification

Positivists including Karl Popper also use an approach called falsification when examining a hypothesis. They ask: 'Can this hypothesis be falsified?' – asking whether there is any evidence to counter the theory. The data is collected and then conclusions drawn to test the theory and establish social facts. (Harvey et al, 2000)

Which methods do positivists prefer?

Positivists generally favour the collection of quantitative data as the most useful for macro-level sociology.

Method	Reasons for preference
Questionnaires	• Can be on a large scale to gain a **representative** sample. • Data collected is **reliable**.
Structured interviews	• Allows the interviewer contact with the respondent, which can eliminate problems such as misunderstanding the questions. • Data collected is **reliable** and **quantitative**.
Official statistics	• Data collected is **quantitative** and **reliable**. • Wide range of data readily available, for example Census data.

Although positivists tend to favour structured methods, note that it is the *aim* of the study, not the *methods*, which tells us that the research is positivist. A positivist would aim to find out *why* divorce rates are high, for example. An interpretivist would aim to find out how individuals *experience* divorce: what are their feelings about it?

Think about ...

Why are interpretivists critical of positivist research?

References

BRYMAN, A. (2012) *Social Research Methods*. 4th Ed. Oxford: Oxford University Press.

DURKHEIM, E. (1951) *Suicide*. New York: Free Press.

HARVEY, L., MACDONALD, M. & HILL, J. (2000) *Theories and Methods*. London: Hodder and Stoughton.

WEBB, R., WESTERGAARD, H., TROBE, K. & STEEL, L. (2009) *A2 Sociology*. Brentwood: Napier Press.

See also: Functionalism; Quantitative data; Reliability; Representativeness; Social facts.

Postmodernism

Postmodernists argue that the modern age has ended and that we now live in postmodern times ('post' meaning 'after'). This may seem confusing because outside of Sociology the present day is often referred to as 'modern times', so how can society be past this? However, sociologists would probably argue that modern times can be characterised by the period following the Industrial Revolution and society has changed considerably since then.

Postmodern theory

The theory focuses on relativism: the view that there is no such thing as an objective truth. The postmodernist Jean-François Lyotard (1984) believed that one theory alone cannot explain the social world. Postmodernists state that society has gone through so much change since industrialisation that traditional 'grand theories' or meta narratives that seek to explain the whole of society like Marxism and functionalism are outdated. Three key words for understanding postmodern theory are: change, diversity and choice.

Change
Postmodernists state that society has become more complex since deindustrialisation. Many people will have several different jobs in their lifetime. They are also less likely to live in the same town all their lives. Relationships also change; statistics published in 2012 estimate that 42 per cent of marriages in England and Wales end in divorce (ONS, 2012). Postmodernists do not make moral judgements about change in society but instead are more likely to see change as progress.

Diversity
For postmodernists there is no value consensus or agreement about how people should live their lives. Instead, there is a diversity of values and lifestyles in

society. Such diversity is the result of multiculturalism and the rise of consumerism.

Choice

In a postmodern society, people feel less pressure to follow traditional norms regarding relationships. People are free to choose their identities, and can change their minds. The rise in megastore supermarkets, large shopping malls and internet shopping means a huge choice of consumer goods. Postmodernists believe that just as individuals have a wide range of consumer choice, so do they have a lot of choices about their relationships and lifestyles.

Pakulski and Waters

In their book *The Death of Class* (1996), Jan Pakulski and Malcolm Waters argued that traditional class identities based on an individual's occupation were becoming less important in society. They argued that since deindustrialisation and the loss of traditional working-class jobs such as mining, people felt less of a collective class identity. Pakulski and Waters claimed that a more individualised society had emerged. Individuals based their identities not on how they *earned* their money, but instead on how they *spent* their money.

Baudrillard

For Jean Baudrillard, society today is characterised by a blurring of reality and simulation. He argued that signs mask reality and obscure them to the extent that they bear no relation to reality because there is no reality. Society is based on hyperreality: the copy but without an original.

Baudrillard discussed simulacra: an image made as a representation of something but only on a superficial level. Contemporary examples include the use of Photoshop on pictures of celebrities in magazines; the celebrity is easily identifiable, but does not look exactly like the edited picture.

Strengths and weaknesses of the theory

Strengths	Weaknesses
• Society has gone through major change since deindustrialisation. Postmodernism reflects these changes; e.g. traditional manual jobs have declined and consumer culture has risen. • While some macro theories are accused of determinism, postmodernism recognises the free will of individuals. • The theory might encourage tolerance of differences due to its focus on diversity.	• Class remains a feature of British society. Lifestyle 'choices' are affected by economic constraint; the individual needs money to buy consumer goods and this ability is based on class. • Postmodernists lack evidence and base their work on assertions, e.g. class is dead and there is no such thing as reality. • Positivists state that 'truth' is an objective fact. It is therefore possible to have one truth. Not all ideas are equally valid in their own way; some are backed by evidence and others are not.

Think about ...

Do you agree that 'grand theories' such as functionalism and Marxism are no longer relevant to society?

See also:
Consumer culture; Social class.

References

BAUDRILLARD, J. (1994) *Simulacra and Simulation*. Translated by GLASER, S. F. Michigan: University of Michigan Press.

LYOTARD, J.-F. (1984) *The Postmodern Condition: A Report on Knowledge*. Manchester: Manchester University Press.

OFFICE FOR NATIONAL STATISTICS (2012) What percentage of marriages end in divorce? [Online] Available from: http://www.ons.gov.uk/ons/rel/vsob1/divorces-in-england-and-wales/sty-what-percentage-of-marriages-end-in-divorce.html. [Accessed: 7th March 2013].

PAKULSKI, J. & WATERS, M. (1996) *The Death of Class*. London: Sage Publications.

Poverty

There is no single agreed definition of poverty. Some definitions focus on lacking basic necessities for survival such as food and shelter, whereas others are based on standards of living compared to others in society. Being in poverty has a significant detrimental effect on an individual's life chances. A myth about poverty is the idea that it is only a problem in 'third world' countries'. In reality many people in the UK are also in poverty.

The Welfare State

In 1945 the then Labour government implemented the Welfare State following recommendations from William Beveridge. In Beveridge's report, poverty (described as 'Want') was one of the 'Five Giant Evils' that the Welfare State was designed to eradicate (along with Squalor, Ignorance, Idleness and Disease). The Welfare State represented a significant change in society, providing a safety net for those who could not work. While the Welfare State arguably smoothed out the sharpest edges of poverty, the gap between rich and poor remained. In fact in 2007–2008 the gap was bigger than at any time since the end of the Second World War. (Hills et al, 2010)

Definitions of poverty

1   Absolute poverty

An individual can be said to be in absolute poverty if they have insufficient money to meet their basic needs such as food, shelter and health care. Absolute poverty is, in theory, measured objectively on the same standard for everyone. It is about determining the very minimum an individual can survive on. Joseph Rowntree measured poverty by determining the minimum income that was needed to buy a weekly 'basket of goods' made up of necessities only, such as food and money for heating bills. It is generally accepted that people in the UK don't live in absolute poverty; however, the growth of food banks across the UK might be a challenge to this view. In addition, some pensioners face the dilemma of whether to 'heat or eat' due to rising costs of fuel. (Beatty et al, 2011)

2   Relative poverty

Not being able to afford things that most people in the UK have would suggest that someone is relatively poor. Relative poverty is difficult to define because it is based on subjective judgements. In the UK, the government's relative measure of poverty is households with an income that falls below 60 per cent of the median income. (PSE, UK)

In 2013, an average of one in five children in the UK lives below the poverty line. In some areas of large cities, this figure rises to 40 per cent (End Child Poverty, 2013). This is an example of relative poverty as it is compared to other children in the UK.

The relative approach was put forward by Peter Townsend in 1979. He devised a deprivation index of 12 items he considered to be important. If an individual did not have these items they were said to be in poverty. In addition to cooked meals, the list included going out with friends and relatives, having a holiday and children's birthday parties. From his index, Townsend claimed that approximately 15 million people were living in poverty. Townsend's work has been criticised for subjective judgements about what items are important and these will, of course, change over time; for example, one of the 12 items listed is a cooked breakfast, but most people today don't regularly eat these. The inclusion of social needs rather than just physical ones, however, was important in changing perceptions of what is meant by poverty.

Poverty in the 21st century

➤ In 2011, 22.7 per cent of the UK population were considered to be at risk of poverty or social exclusion, equivalent to 14 million people. (ONS, 2013)

➤ Every day over 25,000 people around the world die from hunger (UN News Centre, 2009) yet there is enough food in the world for everyone to eat adequately.

➤ Excluding pensioners, in 2011 in the UK there were more households in poverty with people working than not working (6.1 million compared to 5.1 million). (Aldridge et al, 2012)

How can poverty be explained?

There are many explanations of poverty. There are negative perceptions of the poor based on behavioural rather than structural causes of poverty. Charles Murray, for example, researched who he called the 'underclass' and argued controversially that for these people the problem was that they wouldn't work rather than couldn't work. The neo-Marxist Jim Kincaid, however, argues that poverty exists because it benefits the bourgeoisie, who profit from the low wages and long hours of their workers. The rich are only rich because of the poor and the poor are only poor because of the rich; they are co-dependent conditions.

Think about ...

Read the examples below. Who would you consider to be in poverty?

➤ Stephanie has paid her bills for the month, but cannot afford a night out with friends.

See also:
Life chances;
Social mobility;
Underclass.

➤ Fred is a pensioner who is struggling to pay for heating and food, so he often switches his central heating off in winter.

➤ Sarbjit works full-time. Over half of her salary goes towards paying off credit card debts.

References

ALDRIDGE, H., KENWAY, P., MACINNES, T. & PAREKH, A. (2012) *Monitoring Poverty and Social Exclusion 2012.* Joseph Rowntree Foundation. 26th November. [Online] Available from: http://www.jrf.org.uk/publications/monitoring-poverty-2012. [Accessed: 17th March 2013].

BEATTY, T., CROSSLEY, T. & BLOW, L. (2011) *Is there a 'heat or eat' trade-off in the UK?* Institute for Fiscal Studies. Economic and Social Research Council. [Online] Available from: http://www.nuffieldfoundation.org/sites/default/files/files/Is%20there%20a%20heat%20or%20eat%20trade-off%20in%20the%20UK_IFS%20Working%20Paper. [Accessed: 15th March 2013].

END CHILD POVERTY (2013) *Child Poverty Map of the UK.* [Online] Available from: http://www.endchildpoverty.org.uk/images/ecp/130212%20ECP%20local%20report%20final(2).pdf. [Accessed: 17th March 2013].

HILLS, J. et al (2010) *An Anatomy of Economic Inequality in the UK – Summary: Report of the National Equality Panel.* London: Centre for Analysis of Social Exclusion. London School of Economics and Political Science.

OFFICE FOR NATIONAL STATISTICS (2013) *Poverty and Social Exclusion in the UK and EU, 2005–2011.* [Online] Available from: http://www.ons.gov.uk/ons/rel/household-income/poverty-and-social-exclusion-in-the-uk-and-eu/2005-2011/rpt--poverty-and-social-exclusion.html. [Accessed: 17th March 2013].

TOWNSEND, P. (1979) *Poverty in the United Kingdom: A Survey of Household Resources and Standards of Living.* California: University of California Press.

UNITED NATIONS NEWS CENTRE (2009) New UN website aims to educate youth on hunger issues. [Online] Available from: http://www.un.org/apps/news/story.asp?NewsID=30995&Cr=wfp&Cr1=. [Accessed: 4th March 2013].

Qualitative data

Qualitative data is data expressed in word form. It differs from quantitative data which is presented as numbers. Methods that typically collect qualitative data include unstructured interviews, diaries and participant observation. Qualitative data is rich, in-depth data focusing on participants' experiences, thoughts and feelings.

Interpretivists and qualitative data

Interpretivists prefer to use qualitative data as it allows them to gain insight into a person's or group's experiences from a micro level; they are looking at interactions on a more individual level, rather than making generalisations about the whole of society. They reject the scientific method of research, seeing it as cold and detached. Interpretivists are instead interested in gaining empathy and Verstehen with research participants.

Methods producing qualitative data

Primary research	
Overt and covert participant observation	The researcher either overtly (the participants are aware they are being researched) or covertly (participants are unaware) observes the participants in order to collect qualitative, valid data about their behaviour.
Unstructured interviews	An interview is conducted but the questions are not fixed. This allows the researcher to extend questioning in order to collect more data which reflects the respondent's feelings and attitudes.
Secondary research	
Diaries, letters and other personal documents	A researcher uses personal documents to gain an insight into a person or group, as this will give a true and unbiased reflection of their attitudes and values. They may use these in conjunction with a method of primary research to gain a more complete picture (triangulation).

Adler's drug dealer study

Patricia Adler (1985, cited in Bryman, 1988) used qualitative research methods to study drug dealers in California. She spent six years engaging in daily participant observations of the group, with whom she became 'friends'. As well as casually observing them, she also conducted in-depth interviews which continued after she left the group. Her aim was to understand and analyse this deviant social scene by seeing the world from their perspective. It was therefore an ethnographic approach. She was able to gain a detailed insight not only into their hedonistic subculture but also into the businesslike nature of some of their dealings.

Throughout her study, the subjects remained the focal point, and as such the sample did not remain constant as people joined and moved away from the group. The study also centred on her varying relationships with different individuals and what they felt was important about their lives. Since her focus was grounded in perceptions of social reality, Adler's research was clearly a prime example of qualitative data-driven research.

Think about ...

Explain why positivists might criticise research that is based entirely on qualitative data.

See also:
Interpretivism;
Quantitative data;
Triangulation;
Validity;
Verstehen.

References

BRYMAN, A. (1988) *Quantity and Quality in Social Research*. London: Unwin Hyman.

HOWARD GRIFFIN, J. (2004) *Black Like Me: The Definitive Griffin Estate Edition*. Texas: Wings Press.

WEBB, R., WESTERGAARD, H., TROBE, K. & STEEL, L. (2008) *AS Sociology*. Brentwood: Napier Press.

Quantitative data

Quantitative data refers to any data which is presented in a numerical form, such as statistics. In sociological research, these types of results can be extremely useful for identifying common trends in the attitudes and behaviours which are present in society.

Positivists and quantitative data

Positivists tend to prefer collecting quantitative data as it gives an overview of trends in society on a larger scale. Furthermore, quantitative data tends to be more **representative** and **reliable**, which gives a more informed insight into 'social facts'.

Quantitative data allows a researcher to study the wider population; for example, large numbers of people can be surveyed using an online or postal questionnaire. However, these tend to be lacking in **validity** and a method such as a questionnaire doesn't allow the researcher to build a relationship with the respondents. (Webb et al, 2009)

Methods producing quantitative data

Primary research	
Questionnaires	Questionnaires can be easily distributed on a large scale to a **representative** sample. They generally contain closed questions and therefore the results are easy to analyse and turn into quantitative data.
Structured interviews	A researcher may use this technique as it would be possible to build a greater rapport with the subject than if using a questionnaire. This would avoid problems such as the misunderstanding of questions. The questions would be structured so that data gathered would be reliable and easily quantifiable.

Secondary research	
Official statistics	Some sociologists may choose to refer to official statistics to aid their research; these could include government publications, Census data and crime statistics. They might use this data in conjunction with their own primary research to help inform and test their hypothesis, or to give a more informed insight into a larger portion of society if their own research was small-scale.

Hirschi's delinquency study

To conduct his research into the causes of delinquency, Travis Hirschi (1969, cited in Bryman, 1988) surveyed 5,545 school children in California. He distributed a questionnaire (self-completed) to the students, who were carefully chosen to include a representative sample of the schools in the area, gender and race. He also collected data from the schools relating to the children's academic records and used this in conjunction with the findings of the questionnaire. Hirschi's research was clearly focused on his hypothesis; thus with the questions suited exactly to his purpose, he was able to collect large amounts of useful data.

Think about ...

Devise a set of questions that could be used in a questionnaire to enable a researcher to collect quantitative data on the subject of anti-social behaviour.

See also:
Positivism; Reliability; Representativeness; Triangulation; Validity.

References

BRYMAN, A. (1988) *Quantity and Quality in Social Research*. London: Unwin Hyman.

BRYMAN, A. (2012) *Social Research Methods*. 4th Ed. Oxford: Oxford University Press.

WEBB, R., WESTERGAARD, H., TROBE, K. & STEEL, L. (2009) *A2 Sociology*. Brentwood: Napier Press.

Reliability

In sociological terms, the reliability of data refers to whether or not the data is being collected in the same way each time and will produce results which can be replicated. Data can be considered broadly reliable if the same, or similar, results can be gained by different researchers asking the same questions of the same, or similar, people. (Livesey, 2002)

What makes data reliable?

In scientific research, data is considered reliable if other researchers, using the same methods to test the same material, produce equivalent results. Experiments are usually relatively easy to replicate in order to check for consistency of results. If the results are consistent, the researcher can draw generalisations.

In sociological research the same degree of reliability is almost impossible to obtain due to the nature of the subject; however, a standard of reliability can be achieved (Haralambos & Holborn, 2000). For example, if school data is being studied, the researcher may check whether all schools measure exam statistics using the same techniques. They would also look to standardise the research, for example by ensuring that all interviewees are asked the same set of questions in the same order.

Which methods are reliable?

Methods producing quantitative data generate more reliable data than qualitative methods. The outcome is data in a statistical form which can be relatively easily analysed to gain numerical results, such as percentages of a population. The research can also be repeated; this replicability increases the reliability of the data collected. Using a method such as questionnaires can provide a researcher with large amounts of reliable data in a cheap and quick way; for example, a postal or online questionnaire about attitudes towards young offenders could easily be distributed to a large representative sample and the result could be quantified into the percentage of people who thought 'x'. By contrast, with an unstructured group interview, the responses cannot be quantified in the same way and the method would be much harder to replicate.

Anthony Heath – social identities

Anthony Heath et al (2007) set out to investigate whether or not traditional social identities had declined in the UK. A key area of focus was the importance of social class in determining behaviour and attitudes. Heath contributed questions to the British Social Attitudes Survey 2005, some of them repeated from the 1964 British Election study in order to make comparisons over time. The survey included a structured interview and a questionnaire. As each respondent answered exactly the same questions, Heath et al were able to collect reliable data. They concluded from their data that class had become less significant as a source of identity.

Think about ...

A sociologist plans to conduct some research using an online questionnaire. The aim of the study is to find out teenagers' attitudes to drinking. A representative sample of people is selected, which includes an age range from teenagers upwards.

Would this study generate reliable data? Why?

See also:
Qualitative data;
Quantitative data;
Representativeness;
Validity.

References

HARALAMBOS, M. & HOLBORN, M. (2000) *Sociology: Themes and Perspectives*. 5th Ed. London: HarperCollins Publishers.

HEATH, A. F. et al (2007) *Who do we think we are? The decline of traditional class identities*. London: Sage Publications.

LIVESEY, C. (2002) *Reliability*. [Online] Available from: http://www. sociology.org.uk/revision_reliability.pdf.

Representativeness

Research can be considered representative if the sample used accurately reflects the characteristics of the target population. The sample is selected from the target population. The target population rarely means the entire population of the UK; for example, if researching student attitudes towards the rise in university tuition fees, the target population will be university and college students.

Sampling

When research is representative, generalisations can be made. Sampling is necessary in research because, unless the target population is very small, it is impractical or impossible to study everyone. To be representative, a sample needs to be selected from a sampling frame, which is an up-to-date list of the target population.

Target and topic of research	Example of sampling frame
Football fans' views on the price of season tickets	Football clubs' lists of season ticket holders
The attitudes of the general public towards a proposed cap on benefits	The electoral roll (the Census is not a sampling frame for the general public despite being a list of the population of households in Britain, as the data is only collected every 10 years and the information is anonymous for 100 years)

Random samples

Simple random
This is where everyone on the sampling frame has an equal chance of being selected. The word 'random' is sometimes used today to mean haphazard, but remember that asking anyone who happens to be available to take part in a study is *not* random sampling. This is opportunity sampling and is not recommended as the participants do not reflect the target population, so generalisations cannot be made.

Strength – there is no bias in the selection process.

Weakness – some groups could be over- or underrepresented as everyone has an equal chance of being selected; it is possible, though not probable, that from a sampling frame of 50 males and 50 females, 40 males could be selected.

Systematic
Every *n*th person on the sampling frame is selected; this might be every 10th or every 100th person.

Strength – it is easy to use and covers an even spread of a large sampling frame.

Weakness – as with simple random sampling, the over- or underrepresentation of certain groups is possible.

Stratified
Groups appear in the same ratio as in the population from which the sample is selected. For example, in a college 30 per cent of students are white, 20 per cent are black and 50 per cent are Asian. In a sample of 100 students, 30 would be white, 20 black and 50 Asian.

Strength – it overcomes the problem of over- or underrepresentation of certain groups.

Weakness – sometimes a sampling frame does not contain enough information to split the list into groups. In the example above, if the researcher wants to control for ethnicity but only has names to go on, it would involve invalid guesswork. Also, sometimes a sampling frame is not available. This is usually the case in hidden populations, such as illegal drug users and homeless people. A non-random sampling technique will need to be used.

Non-random samples

Snowball
This sampling technique is based on personal contacts. Just as a snowball gets bigger as it rolls down a hill, a snowball

sample gets bigger as one person puts the researcher in touch with another, and so on.

Strength – it is useful for topics such as criminal gangs where it is difficult for non-members to gain access.

Weakness – the researcher is relying on their one contact to put them in touch with others, so have lost control of their sample. Just like a snowball rolling down a hill, the researcher doesn't know when the sampling will stop.

Purposive

The sample is deliberately chosen (or chosen on purpose) for being useful and knowledgeable about the topic being studied. Purposive sampling is often used at the pilot stage of research (a trial run).

Strength – it is very useful when the participants know more about the topic being studied than the researcher does, so that new information can be learned to assist the research; for example, researching a new religious movement to which the researcher does not belong.

Weakness – the sample is chosen for its subject knowledge so is unlikely to reflect the target population.

Poor response rates

This is a particular problem with postal questionnaires; the researcher might send out thousands, but will not get a representative sample if few are returned. To try to overcome this problem, researchers might offer an incentive such as entry into a prize draw.

Think about ...

Give four examples of hidden populations for which a sampling frame does not exist.

See also:
Reliability;
Validity.

Reserve army of labour

A reserve army of labour is a Marxist concept used to describe a group of people who are brought into the labour market on a temporary basis at times of economic boom. For Karl Marx, they are an exploited group, hired and fired at the will of the bourgeoisie or ruling class.

A reserve army of labour either have no contracts or are working on temporary contracts. Marxists say this means they are more likely to have poor pay and poor conditions. Being temporary, they are unlikely to join a trade union, so not only are their own jobs unprotected, but the union action of permanent employees is weakened by having fewer members.

Women

During the Second World War, women became a reserve army of labour when men were called up to fight. They worked in jobs that had previously been considered unsuitable for women, including mechanics and engineering. However, after the war, the men resumed their jobs and most women were expected to return to being housewives. This was arguably exploiting the skills of women who had spent years mastering a trade.

According to the Marxist feminist Irene Bruegel, while women by the 1970s had benefited from an increase in employment opportunities, they were still more vulnerable to redundancy than men and therefore the reserve army of labour theory still applied. (Bruegel, 1979)

Migrant workers

Workers can sometimes be found more cheaply from other countries. They become a reserve army of labour as they might be working temporarily in the UK. Some newspapers then give readers the idea that 'they are coming over here and stealing our jobs'. Marxists argue that this is deliberate; the bourgeoisie have set up the white working class to blame the migrant workers instead of blaming the bourgeoisie. Migrant workers then become a convenient scapegoat because a division among the proletariat (the workers) prevents them from taking collective action against the bourgeoisie.

An example of the exploitation of a reserve army of labour came in 2004 when 23 Chinese workers drowned while cockle-picking in Morecambe Bay. It is believed they were employed by a criminal gang, were due to be paid very little and were not trained to be working in such dangerous conditions (quicksand and rising tides).

Does the concept still apply today?

The concept is less applicable today than in the 1800s when Marx was writing, as legislation to protect workers has improved. The 2010 Equality Act protects workers on many grounds, including age, gender and ethnicity. However, at a time of recession, some workers feel afraid to speak up about poor working conditions. The concept does still therefore retain its relevance.

Think about ...

In what ways do students form a reserve army of labour?

See also:
Feminism;
Marxism.

References

BRUEGEL, I. (1979) Women as a Reserve Army of Labour: A Note on Recent British Experience. *Feminist Review*. 3. Palgrave Macmillan Journals.

GOV.UK (2013) National minimum wage rates. [Online] Available from: https://www.gov.uk/national-minimum-wage-rates. [Accessed: 11th February 2013].

PAI, H-H. (2012) What happened to the families of the drowned cocklepickers of Morecambe Bay? *The Guardian*. 22nd October. [Online] Available from: http://www.guardian.co.uk/world/2012/oct/22/drowned-chinese-cocklepickers-morecambe-bay. [Accessed: 11th February 2013].

Rites of passage

A rite of passage is an event or milestone which marks a significant change in an individual's life. Many rites of passage mark the transition from childhood or youth to adulthood. In some cultures, rites of passage are recognised by initiation ceremonies but in the UK they are generally more informal markers of change in status.

What are rites of passage?

Rites of passage are social constructions. They vary across religion, culture and time. Many rites of passage will not apply to everyone and the significance of each event will also vary by individual and community.

Rites of passage change over time; for example, an individual's 21st birthday used to mark a transition to adulthood and a time when the individual was considered old enough to have their own home. At 21, the individual was said to have 'the key to the door' (this is why 21st birthday cards often have pictures of keys on the design). It was the age of majority or adulthood. However, 21 was lowered to 18 in 1970, and nowadays 18 is perhaps a more significant milestone.

The following might be considered examples of rites of passage in the UK:

➤ leaving compulsory education

➤ having a serious relationship

➤ moving out of the parents' home

➤ getting a job.

Rites of passage in the UK are somewhat subjective and the lines between childhood, youth and adulthood are blurred. In some cultures, however, these are more formally marked through initiation ceremonies. On the Pacific island of Vanuatu, land diving is a rite of passage.

Once boys have been circumcised at seven or eight years old (a rite of passage in itself), they will participate in their first dive. The boy jumps from a tall tower made from wood tied with vines. Vines are tied to his ankle and he dives to the ground. When a boy dives for the first time, his mother holds an item representing his childhood. As he dives, she throws the item away.

Types of rites of passage

Arnold Van Gennep (2004) identified three types:

1. **Separation:** These are performed at the end of an individual's life. An example is a funeral which helps the family adjust to life after the death of a loved one.

2. **Transition:** This is where the individual learns the norms and values of a new life stage they are entering. It is preparation for a significant life change. For example, becoming engaged might enable a couple to adjust and prepare for married life. Another example is doing an apprenticeship as preparation for a future career.

3. **Incorporation:** This is when the individual has settled into a new role, for example a marriage or a job.

Think about ...

What do you think is the most important milestone in an individual's life? What made you feel that you were an adult, or when do you think you will consider yourself to be an adult?

See also:
Socialisation.

References

VAN GENNEP, A. (2004) *The Rites of Passage*. London: Routledge.

http://listverse.com/2009/12/28/10-bizarre-rites-of-passage.

Roles

Roles are the set of social expectations attached to a position or status. Individuals (or actors) learn how to perform their roles through the socialisation process. Roles provide a template or guideline of how to behave based on an individual's position in society. Most individuals perform many different roles and these will change over their lifetime.

Examples of how roles change

Age	Emma's roles
18	Student, girlfriend, daughter, sister, friend, part-time healthcare assistant
36	Doctor, mother, wife, friend, sister, daughter
72	Volunteer, mother, grandmother, friend, sister, wife, carer

Age	Jerome's roles
18	Apprentice, son, friend, footballer
36	Electrician, father, partner, son, friend, part-time student, football coach
72	Father, grandfather, friend, vice president of a local football club

Role conflict

As people in society perform many different roles, role conflict will be inevitable at times. For example, a student must complete an essay for a deadline, but this conflicts with her role as a friend as there is a birthday party she is expected to attend; a lawyer needs to work late on a difficult case ready for court the next day, but this conflicts with his role as a parent and the homework he will be expected to help with that evening. Life involves juggling different roles.

Role-learning theory

Role-learning theory emphasises that it is through socialisation that individuals learn the expectations attached to their roles in society. Social roles are defined by the culture individuals find themselves in and are therefore largely based on constraint rather than choice.

Society has expectations of what a nurse, lawyer, teacher or parent should do and it is not easy to deviate much from these expectations. People conform to role expectations partly as a result of sanctions and rewards. For example, a student will be expected to work hard in order to achieve good grades; they might be punished for not working well by being given a detention, a disciplinary warning or by failing an exam; or they might be rewarded for conforming to expectations by receiving merit points, certificates or a good grade in an exam.

However, role-learning theory stresses that external constraints only work to a certain extent; to continue to meet role expectations, people must internalise their roles and become committed to them (Fulcher & Scott, 1999). Most students will be more successful if they look beyond rewards and sanctions and work hard because they want to achieve.

Think about ...

Identify the roles you play in society. Give examples of how these roles conflict with each other.

Reference

FULCHER, J. & SCOTT, J. (1999) *Sociology*. Oxford: Oxford University Press.

See also:
Culture;
Deviance;
Norms;
Socialisation;
Values.

Secularisation

Many sociologists believe that society is becoming increasingly secular; that is, that religion is becoming less influential and levels of religiosity lower among members of society.

Bryan Wilson (1966, cited in Aldridge, 2007) defines secularisation as 'The process whereby **religious thinking, practice** and **institutions** lose social significance'. These three areas can help indicate whether or not secularisation is occurring in UK society.

Religious practice: attendance

Statistics clearly show a decline in religious practice in the UK's mainstream churches.

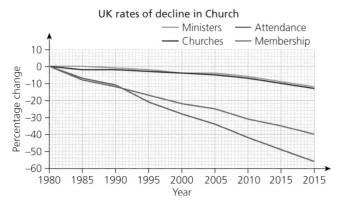

UK rates of decline in Church

Religious institutions: disengagement

Steve Bruce claims that religious institutions are becoming increasingly separate from wider society; this process is called 'disengagement'. For example, at one time the Church was a focal point of communities, but less so today. Talcott Parsons calls this 'structural differentiation' as the Church and other key organisations now perform fewer functions in society; they have a more specialised role rather than a wider-reaching one throughout society. However, the Queen as head of state is also the head of the Church of England, and bishops still sit in the House of

Lords, so it could be argued that religious institutions do still play significant roles in UK society.

Religious thinking: disenchantment

According to Max Weber, people are becoming more reliant on rational thinking, such as scientific discovery, and are disenchanted with beliefs in the supernatural or 'other'. There has been a decline in beliefs in concepts such as heaven, hell, sin and the devil in recent years and society no longer lives in 'fear of God' as in medieval times. Conversely, the British Social Attitudes Survey in 1991 found that 62 per cent of people believed in 'God'. We may criticise the validity of these statistics, however, as a person can *say* they believe in a 'God' but never actually put this into practice.

In the British Social Attitudes survey of 2011, half of all respondents stated that they did not belong to a particular religion. The decline in religion can be explained by 'generational replacement' as the generally more religious older generations die out and are replaced by a less religious population.

Think about ...

Why might some people who do not consider themselves to be religious still tick 'Christian' on the Census?

See also:
New Age
Movements;
NRMs.

References

ALDRIDGE, A. (2007) *Religion in the Contemporary World*. Cambridge: Polity Press.

WEBB, R., WESTERGAARD, H., TROBE, K. & STEEL, L. (2009) *A2 Sociology*. Brentwood: Napier Press.

Self-fulfilling prophecy

A self-fulfilling prophecy is a prediction that causes itself to come true because the belief of an individual creates a change in behaviour.

Examples of self-fulfilling prophecy

Examples of self-fulfilling prophecy include:

➤ A student tells herself and others that she is going to fail an exam. She is stuck in a negative mind-set and does little revision because she is convinced that she will fail anyway. She fails the exam.

➤ A man is convinced that his marriage will fail and his wife will leave him. His negative beliefs and lack of trust put a strain on the marriage and his wife leaves him.

Those examples are negative, but they can also be positive:

➤ If the student in the example above tells herself and others that she will pass the exam, she is likely to behave in a way that increases her chances of being successful; she will do more revision.

Self-fulfilling prophecy and stereotypes

If a group of people are expected to behave in a certain way, they might (or might not) live up to that expected behaviour. Nick Barham observed that the media increasingly demonises young people and that they are being stereotyped as criminals. When the activities that young people want to engage in are labelled as illegal, there are, of course, more young criminals. The tendency to criminalise street culture, such as graffiti, might widen its appeal. (Barham, 2004)

Self-fulfilling prophecy and education

Self-fulfilling prophecies are associated with labelling theory. To a significant extent, individuals' identities are based on their perceptions of how other people see them. They are therefore likely to be influenced by the labels others attach to them.

Robert Rosenthal and Lenore Jacobson researched the impact that teachers' expectations have on the behaviour and academic performance of their pupils. The researchers informed teachers in a primary school that a group of pupils were 'spurters' who were very likely to be high-achieving pupils. In reality, they were selected at random and were therefore of mixed abilities. All pupils completed IQ tests at the beginning and end of the study and the pupils identified as the 'spurters' did make more progress than the rest of the class. Rosenthal and Jacobson stated that this was due to a self-fulfilling prophecy. The 'spurters' were likely to have been given more attention than the rest of the class. They gained in confidence because their teachers saw them as successful and they therefore went on to succeed. (Rosenthal & Jacobson, 1968)

This study, however, was conducted in the 1960s and teacher training today focuses a lot more on equal opportunities in the treatment of students. In addition, labels do not always stick. Students can reject a label; if labelled as a failure, they might work extra hard to prove the label to be wrong.

Self-fulfilling prophecy and deviance

Being labelled a deviant can lead to an amplification of deviance. For example, the London riots in the summer of 2011 received a lot of media focus. Some believe that this led to 'copycat' riots in other cities, including Manchester and Birmingham. Young people were labelled as deviant and some therefore conformed to the label.

In the late 1990s, the government introduced ASBOs (Anti-Social Behaviour Orders) to tackle social problems such as vandalism and drunken behaviour. The order restricts those issued with an ASBO from going to a particular place or spending time with people who are known as troublemakers. Although anyone deemed to be behaving anti-socially could be issued with an ASBO, the majority are given to young people. They are viewed as a 'badge of honour' by some recipients. A report by the Institute for Public Policy Research has criticised the use of ASBOs for labelling young people as criminal and fast-tracking them into a life of crime. ASBOs arguably become self-fulfilling prophecies. (IPPR, 2007)

Labels do affect outcomes but it is important to stress the factors outside of a person's control. A student will not become a doctor without the necessary academic qualifications, regardless of how much they and their parents want them to succeed. An individual is highly unlikely to have a big win on the lottery, regardless of how much thought they have given to how they would spend the money. While an individual's drive to succeed will be a big factor in their success, a belief that something will happen might not cause it to materialise because of barriers such as money, education and family background.

Think about ...

How have the expectations of you held by your teachers or parents shaped your experiences?

See also:
Symbolic
interactionism.

References

BARHAM, N. (2004) *Disconnected*. London: Random House.

IPPR (2007) ASBO culture making kids criminals. 10th December. [Online] Available from: http://www.ippr.org/press-releases/111/2048/asbo-culture-making-kids-criminals. [Accessed: 27th February 2013].

ROSENTHAL, R. & JACOBSON, L. (1968) *Pygmalion in the Classroom*. New York: Holt, Rinehart and Winston.

Social class

Social class is discussed a lot in the UK but it is difficult to reach agreement about a definition. Some people consider their class to be based on their family background, or their parents' jobs; others think they have no class identity at all. In simple terms, we can state that: social class = occupation + culture. 'Put three Englishmen on a desert island and within an hour they'll have invented a class system.' (Alan Ayckbourn, playwright)

Class confusion

The traditional labels of class perhaps made more sense in Victorian Britain when a coal miner would be identified as working class, a teacher would be middle class, and wealthy landowners (aristocrats) and factory owners made up the tiny but powerful upper class.

Society has seen considerable changes since industrial times when these labels were first used and it is more difficult to apply them to society today. This might explain why different surveys reveal dramatically different results about class identity. For example, a survey by the National Centre for Social Research revealed that 57 per cent of respondents claimed to be working class, yet this percentage exceeds the number of people in jobs that would be considered working class (Womack, 2007). However, in 2012 a survey by Britain Thinks showed that 70 per cent of respondents considered themselves to be middle class (Rentoul & Chorley, 2012). This survey would have had a different sample of respondents, yet the differences in percentages are dramatic.

The death of class

Postmodernists Jan Pakulski and Malcolm Waters claimed that class was dying out as a marker of identity; ethnicity, age and regionality were now becoming more important.

They also state that identity based on social class has been replaced by consumer culture (Pakulski & Waters, 1996).

However, people's ability to buy desirable products does largely depend on their jobs and therefore their class.

The findings of a *Guardian*/ICM poll in 2007 go against the view that we now have a classless society, as 89 per cent of respondents said that they think people are judged by their class (Glover, 2007). And even if class becomes less important as a source of identity, it is still very important as a source of inequality. There is a wide gap between rich and poor in Britain and class is a strong determining factor of an individual's life chances.

Think about ...

Savage and Devine (2013) carried out the largest social class study of all time in the UK and stated that working-, middle- and upper-class labels are outdated. Their findings indicate that there are now seven classes in Britain ranging from an 'elite' at the top to the 'precariat' (the precarious proletariat) at the bottom. Follow the link in the References to find out where you fit in.

See also:
Life chances;
Marxism;
Postmodernism;
Poverty; Social
mobility.

References

BBC NEWS MAGAZINE. (2013) The Great British Class Calculator: What class are you? 3rd April. [Online] Available from: http://www.bbc.co.uk/news/magazine-22000973. [Accessed: 19th May 2013].

GLOVER, J. (2007) Riven by class and no social mobility: Britain in 2007. *The Guardian*. 20th October. [Online] Available from: http://www.guardian.co.uk/uk/2007/oct/20/britishidentity.socialexclusion. [Accessed: 11th December 2012].

PAKULSKI, J. & WATERS, M. (1996) *The Death of Class*. London: Sage Publications.

RENTOUL, J. & CHORLEY, M. (2012) Seven in ten of us belong to middle Britain. Britain Thinks. In FIRTH, L. (ed.) (2012) *Class and Social Mobility*. 219. Cambridge: Independence Educational Publishers.

WOMACK, S. (2007) Rise of the Working Class? In FIRTH, L. (ed.) (2008) *A Classless Society?* 149. Cambridge: Independence Educational Publishers.

Social closure

Social closure is a concept that was used by Max Weber to refer to the means by which a group maintains privileges for its members. It is the process of keeping outsiders out. The term can be applied to gender and ethnicity but is most commonly discussed in relation to social class and how the upper classes maintain their elite position in society.

Social closure and the upper class

The upper class is a powerful elite group in society. The upper class includes aristocracy (landowners with titles) and people who have inherited considerable wealth from their family businesses. They practise social closure in the following ways:

➤ **Education:** Their children are usually educated in public schools. Here they gain access to a level of **cultural capital** that most members of society have not had, for example learning Latin.

➤ **An 'old boys' network':** Through their education, the upper classes are able to network with others who attended public schools. This gives them increased social capital and advantages not available to most people. For example, a significant number of students at Oxford and Cambridge universities went to Eton or Harrow School. Many boys at Eton are the sons of old Etonians. The upper classes are self-recruiting.

➤ **Marriage:** Members of the upper class will typically marry someone of a similar social standing. If they married into the lower classes, they would lose their elite position; marrying within their class enhances the power of both families. For this reason, arranged marriages used to be a common occurrence within the aristocracy.

➤ **Inheritance:** The upper classes pass their money on to their children. Often this is through a family line that goes back hundreds of years; so this is often described as 'old money'. The family seat, often a stately home, is also inherited.

> **Leisure activities:** The upper class has interests which are not easily accessed by the rest of the society, such as fox hunting. This has been a popular pursuit of the upper class since Victorian times. Traditionally, a hunt meets twice a week and the most important one is on Boxing Day. Hunters are expected to conform to a dress code and attend formal social occasions such as a hunt ball.

Exclusionary and usurpationary closure

Frank Parkin (1979) identified two key forms of social closure:

1 Exclusionary closure

This is a means of excluding others by placing barriers in their way so that the group can maintain its existing privileges. Examples include setting public school fees so high that most people can't afford them, having a strict 'members only' policy at a golf club where new members must be recommended by existing members, and fraternities at American universities that require individuals to pass initiation ceremonies.

2 Usurpationary closure

This is a means of attempting to gain the privileges held by others. In Marxist theory, if the proletariat could overthrow the bourgeoisie, this would be an example of usurpationary closure. Further examples include attending marches, joining a trade union and going on strike to improve pay.

Think about ...

In addition to fox hunting, what other leisure activities might the upper class take part in which exclude outsiders?

See also:
Capital;
Social class;
Weberianism.

Reference

PARKIN, F. (1979) *Marxism and Class Theory: A Bourgeois Critique.* London: Tavistock.

Social control

Social control refers to the regulation of human behaviour by society. It is the means of ensuring that individuals conform to the norms of society. Functionalists argue that social control is essential to prevent deviance and to keep society running smoothly. For Marxists, however, social control is exercised to maintain the advantages of the bourgeoisie by keeping the proletariat 'in their place'.

Formal social control

Formal social control refers to the sanctions enforced by the government to prevent instability in society. The law controls behaviour through punishments, which also act as a deterrent to behaviour that is considered undesirable; for example, the threat of a large fine or a prison sentence discourages many people from committing crime.

According to Emile Durkheim, some crime can be functional, due to the ways in which the public react to criminal activity. In the eighteenth century, criminals were publicly executed and local people would cheer at the hanging. Social solidarity was reinforced as collective ideas of right and wrong were reaffirmed. Today, when a crime is reported on television, the news footage often includes people's reactions of disgust or upset in the local community. The viewer is encouraged to sympathise with the victims and to want the criminal to be brought to justice. The reaction to the crime becomes a collective one.

Big Brother is watching you

Today, much of social control is by surveillance. In the novel *1984* by George Orwell, the character Big Brother is a dictator who watches his citizens at all times. The term 'Big Brother' is now used to describe the government watching the public in order to control people.

Examples include CCTV (closed-circuit television) which gives people the sense of always being watched so that they might regulate their own behaviour as a result. Jeremy Bentham designed the panopticon prison which was circular and enabled a prison guard to watch all inmates at all times. The sociologist Michel Foucault argued that this panopticon style applied to the wider society, where people did not need to be locked away to feel like they were being controlled by the state. In 2010, CCTV cameras were installed in two Muslim communities in Birmingham as a counter-terrorism initiative (Lewis, 2010). They were eventually taken down as ethical and legal concerns were raised about civil liberties.

Since 9/11, there has been an increase in social control by surveillance. Most airports have stepped up their security with strict regulations about what can be taken onto planes and many searches of luggage and of the passengers themselves.

Informal social control

Informal social control refers to the ways in which agents of socialisation encourage people to keep to unwritten rules. It is a more subtle form of control but can be just as powerful and affects most people in their daily lives:

Example of social control from agent of socialisation
Peer group: A teenager is ridiculed for wearing unfashionable trainers. He saves up to buy new ones to fit in with his peers.
Mass media: A woman feels fat compared to celebrities in magazines. She follows a published celebrity diet to conform to media ideals about body image.
Family: A father is late home from work and misses his daughter's bedtime story. She is unhappy with him in the morning. He leaves work earlier that day so that he can read to her.

Case study

Stephanie wakes up late and her mother shouts at her to get ready for college. Her image is captured on CCTV on the bus, in the street, and in college before she arrives at her first class. She is given a warning from her teacher for being late. After college, she goes to the shops to buy a dress she has seen advertised in a magazine to wear that night. Her bus ticket is inspected on her journey home. Her friends pressurise her to get drunk on a night out. The next morning she posts pictures of herself and her friends on a social networking site and others comment on them.

The example above shows how an individual might be subject to daily social control, but it is also important to note that individuals have free will. Many people feel freedom as well as constraint in a democratic society and are able to make choices.

Think about ...

'CCTV keeps everyone safe. It does not restrict freedom.' Do you agree with this viewpoint?

See also:
Deviance;
Socialisation.

References

FOUCAULT, M. (1991) *Discipline and Punish: The Birth of the Prison.* Translated by SHERIDAN, A. London: Penguin.

LEWIS, P. (2010) CCTV aimed at Muslim areas in Birmingham to be dismantled. *The Guardian.* 25th October. [Online] Available from: http://www.guardian.co.uk/uk/2010/oct/25/birmingham-cctv-muslim-areas-surveillance. [Accessed: 5th January 2013].

Social facts

Social facts include any way of thinking or acting which is general to society, is external to its individual members and has a constraining influence (Durkheim, 1938). Emile Durkheim argued that Sociology should be treated as a science because of the existence of social facts. He stated that social facts must be seen as 'things' rather than ideas and as such were measurable, observable and could be treated like objects in the natural sciences.

Characteristics of social facts

Durkheim wrote about social facts to show that human behaviour was in many ways predictable and that generalisations could be made about society as a whole. It was therefore necessary to attribute behaviour to the structure of society rather than to the individual alone. The following are characteristics of social facts:

➤ They exist outside of the individual.

➤ They constrain or control the individual.

➤ They are general throughout society, applying to the members as a whole.

Language

Language should be seen as a social fact because it fulfils the characteristics above:

➤ It exists outside of the individual and prior to the individual.

➤ It is general because normally members of the same society or community will speak the same language.

➤ It is constraining because the rules of grammar have to be observed in order to be understood.

Language is always evolving, with some words going out of fashion and new slang created. However, this does not prevent language from being a social fact. Language still has an external reality to the individual and Durkheim acknowledged that social facts change over time.

Suicide

Although suicide may seem to be a highly individual act, according to Durkheim the causes of suicide rates can be found in the structure of society. He studied suicide rates in European countries and found that there were considerable differences between groups. Trends were therefore identifiable:

➤ Unmarried people had a higher rate of suicide than married people.

➤ Suicide was more prevalent among those who lived in the city than those who lived in the countryside.

➤ Suicide rates were higher among Protestants than Catholics.

If the causes of suicide were down to the psychological state of the individual alone, Durkheim would not have been able to spot such patterns; he had therefore identified social facts. Social facts are vital in challenging the view that behaviour is all down to the individual's own choices. Durkheim's work can be criticised as people do have free will, but much of behaviour can be explained by social influences.

Think about ...

Research the contributions made by Auguste Comte to your understanding of social facts.

See also:
Functionalism;
Positivism;
Sociological
imagination.

References

DURKHEIM, E. (1897) 2002 *Suicide: A Study in Sociology*. London: Routledge.

DURKHEIM, E. (1895) 1938 *The Rules of Sociological Method*. New York: Free Press.

Socialisation

Socialisation is the process by which an individual learns the norms and values of society. Through socialisation, common norms and values are passed on from one generation to the next to ensure that society operates effectively. Without socialisation, there is very little that an individual can do; even the most basic behaviour and everyday tasks that seem almost automatic have to be learned.

Stages of socialisation

Primary socialisation is the learning of basic norms and values that are required to survive in society, including how to dress and feed yourself, and saying 'please' and 'thank you'. Primary socialisation lays the foundations for the rest of an individual's life. The family (parents in particular) have the main influence in this crucial stage of socialisation, which lasts until the age of four or five when the child has more encounters with other influences.

Secondary socialisation is all the learning that takes place throughout the rest of the individual's life. The socialisation process never stops; people continue to learn new things. The family remains important, but so too are education, the peer group, the mass media, religion and work.

During the process of socialisation identities are formed. These include class, age, gender and ethnic identities.

Agents of socialisation

The agents of socialisation are the institutions and people that influence the learning of society's culture. The following are the main agents:

Family
As most people are raised by a family and it is the primary agent of socialisation, it arguably has the strongest influence. Even if an individual later rebels, the influence is likely to endure.

➤ For young children, basic norms are learned by copying the behaviour of parents and older siblings who act as role models.

➤ Parents have a significant role in the gendering of their children through the toys they buy, the colour clothes they dress them in and the language used.

➤ A child learns their ethnic identity from the family; parents and grandparents play a key role in keeping third generation children from minority ethnic backgrounds in touch with their 'roots'.

➤ Class identities are strongly influenced by the family, so much so that people in professional occupations such as doctors might consider themselves to be working class because their grandfather was a miner!

Education
The education system has an important role in the socialisation process.

➤ Unlike other agents of socialisation, education is compulsory.

➤ In addition to learning the formal curriculum, including maths, English and science, students are exposed to a hidden curriculum.

➤ Some students resist the influence of school, particularly during compulsory education; for example, in Paul Willis's study (1977) the 'lads' resisted school rules, rejected the authority of their teachers and saw school as a place to have a laugh with friends. However, Willis's research was carried out in the 1970s when it was easier to get a job without formal qualifications than it is today.

➤ The labour market has changed and young people are spending longer in education than ever before. There has also been a growth in lifelong learning.

Peer group

This includes friends and others of a similar age and social position.

➤ During adolescence, most people become increasingly independent from parents and the influence of the peer group becomes more profound. A young person might not care if their father does not like their clothes, but might be hurt if their friends express similar views.

➤ Peer pressure can lead young people to engage in behaviour that is normally viewed as negative, such as misbehaving in school, drinking and drug-taking. However, the peer group is vital in supporting young people in their transition from childhood to adulthood.

➤ Today, there is a growing trend for people in their 20s and 30s to live with friends, so the peer group may retain its influence for longer.

Mass media

The mass media plays a key role in socialisation and is a significant part of the daily life of most people. However, the media is a two-way process; through social networking, people shape and influence the media themselves. Many young people have YouTube accounts where they upload videos which in turn influence others.

It is difficult to determine how far people are influenced by the media and today the idea that it has a direct influence on behaviour is disputed. When people first had televisions back in the 1950s and 1960s, audiences had a more passive role and were surprised by its content. Today, however, people are more media-savvy and direct influences may have reduced.

Religion

For many people in the UK, religion is an important agent of socialisation. For example, the word Islam means 'way of life' so for most practising Muslims, religion has a strong influence on their norms and values. However, society has become increasingly secular; religion is in decline.

➤ A Tearfund Survey found that only 7 per cent of the population identified as practising Christians. (Ashworth, 2007)

➤ In the 2001 Census, 15 per cent of respondents said they have no religion compared to 25 per cent in 2011. The number of atheists may be greater than these figures suggest as some people may tick a religion because their parents are Hindu or Christian, or because they were christened in a church as a baby, but have little attachment to the faith.

However, for atheists living in an increasingly secular society, religion still has an influence; for example, they are still likely to take part in religious festivals such as Christmas, even without religious belief.

Work
Much of our lives is spent in work and many young people today can expect to be working into their 70s. Work is therefore central to many people's sense of self. Today, many workers change jobs several times before they are 30. They are therefore continually adapting to different work cultures. In an unstable job market with less job security and the threat of redundancy, people in their 50s and older are retraining and learning new skills rather than 'winding down' to retirement.

Influence on behaviour

While agents of socialisation have a significant influence on behaviour, the level of influence is difficult to determine. People are not like chemicals in a laboratory; they cannot easily be isolated from other agents of socialisation to determine the effects of each one; for example, there is concern that violence in the media leads to violent behaviour, and that seeing pictures of skinny models leads to eating disorders. However, most people who play violent computer games or read celebrity magazines don't exhibit these behaviours. When they do, it could instead be due to the influence of peers, the family or genetics. We can therefore assume that the influence of each agent of socialisation differs according to the individual.

Think about ...

Parents socialise their children, but children also socialise their parents. Give examples of how this occurs.

References

ASHWORTH, J. (2007) *Churchgoing in the UK: A research report from Tearfund on church attendance in the UK*. Middlesex: Tearfund.

OFFICE FOR NATIONAL STATISTICS (2012) Religion in England and Wales 2011. [Online] Available from: http://www.ons.gov.uk/ons/rel/census/2011-census/key-statistics-for-local-authorities-in-england-and-wales/rpt-religion.html. [Accessed: 2nd February 2013].

WILLIS, P. (1977) *Learning to Labour: How Working Class Kids Get Working Class Jobs*. Farnborough: Saxon House.

See also: Culture; Hidden curriculum; Nature versus nurture; Norms; Values.

Social mobility

Social mobility refers to movement between social positions or classes. The term is usually used for upward mobility rather than downward mobility. Individuals can be considered upwardly mobile if they are in a higher social position than that of their parents.

Social mobility can be seen as a sign of a fair society.

Perceptions about social mobility

Consider this example: Noel's father is a bricklayer and his mother a shop assistant. He has good exam results and goes to university. After his degree and postgraduate study, he begins a professional occupation as a solicitor. Noel marries another professional and has effectively become middle class. How realistic is Noel's story? Social mobility may actually be in decline.

A British Social Attitudes (BSA) report in 2010 revealed that people feel they have experienced upward mobility; that they have reached a higher level in their careers than their parents did. The results showed that 39 per cent felt they had a higher-level occupation than their fathers, whereas only 23 per cent thought they were in a lower-level occupation. Of the people who took part in the survey, 84 per cent said that hard work was important to achieve upward mobility. Only 14 per cent said that being born into a wealthy family was important to get on in life. (Heath et al, 2012)

Social mobility today

The findings of the BSA report suggest that respondents considered society to be meritocratic. However, researchers from the University of California claim that social mobility is now slower than it was in medieval England. Professor Gregory Clark et al traced the levels of intergenerational mobility of people with a 'rich' surname and those with a 'poor' surname from 1858 to 2011. Those with the rich surname were still considerably richer than those with the poor surname over 150 years on. However, the rate of upward mobility in the Middle Ages was surprisingly better. In 1350, 'Smith' was very much a working-class name. However, by 1650 there were as many 'Smiths' in the wealthiest 1 per cent of the country as in the population as a whole, suggesting that they had become part of the elite. (Dunt, 2011)

Social mobility and education

Education offers the best chance of upward social mobility. However, children from working-class and middle-class backgrounds start school in very different positions and the achievement gap gets bigger throughout their time in school. Just 21 per cent of the poorest fifth of children attained five good GCSEs (grades A*–C) in 2012, compared to 75 per cent of the wealthiest fifth. (ESRC, 2011)

Think about ...

Compare the jobs of your parents to the jobs held by your grandparents. Was social mobility observable? What are your predictions for your generation of the family?

See also: Life chances; NEETs; Social class; Social closure.

References

DUNT, I. (2011) Social mobility 'slower than in medieval England'. 4th April. [Online] Available from: http://www.politics.co.uk/news/2011/04/04/social-mobility-slower-than-in-medieval-england. [Accessed: 9th February 2013].

ECONOMIC & SOCIAL RESEARCH COUNCIL (2011) Education vital for social mobility. [Online] Available from: http://www.esrc.ac.uk/_images/education-vital-social-mobility_tcm8-20069.pdf. [Accessed: 10th February 2013].

HEATH, A., DE GRAAF, N. D. & LI, Y. (2012) How fair is the route to the top? In Firth, L. (ed.) (2012) Class and Social Mobility. Cambridge: Independence Educational Publishers.

Sociological imagination

The phrase 'sociological imagination' was coined by Charles Wright Mills in 1959 to describe the importance of the ability to link the individual to the society. Having a sociological imagination means that individuals can think beyond their own situation and relate their experiences to the wider society. Mills wrote his ideas in his book, *The Sociological Imagination*, a text widely read by students studying Sociology at university.

The problem

Mills wrote that many people feel trapped in their lives, but that they don't tend to see their problems as being a result of the wider society. Most people struggle to cope with personal difficulties because they do not understand the structure of society that lies behind their problems. Mills argued that the rate of change was so fast that it outpaced the individual's ability to adapt their norms and values to new circumstances.

The solution

Mills argued that gaining a sociological imagination would enable people to develop reason in order to understand what is going on in the world and what is happening within themselves. He believed that it was important to avoid sticking to one 'grand theory' to explain society and instead to be aware of how society is constantly changing. Mills wanted Sociology to be more than an academic subject – he wanted it to be used to address inequality in society: 'The sociological imagination has its chance to make a difference in the quality of human life in our time.' (Mills, 1959)

Using a sociological imagination

> ➤ **Unemployment:** Mills argues that if one man in an entire city is unemployed, then that would be his

personal problem and it would be acceptable to look to his characteristics to explain why he does not have a job. However, if in a country 10 per cent of the population of working age do not have a job, then it is now due to the structure of society – recession, for example.

➤ **Marriage:** A wife and husband may experience personal difficulties, but an estimated 40 per cent of marriages now end in divorce and the marriage rate in 2009 was at its lowest since records began (ONS, 2011). Therefore, this cannot be blamed on the individual problems of the couple, but instead must be due to the structure of society.

➤ **Underachievement in education:** If an individual student is the only one in the class to fail a course because they did not submit their coursework, failure can be attributed to the individual. However, when we know that approximately 40 per cent of the entire GCSE cohort do not achieve five passes graded A*–C, this cannot be explained by the individual efforts of the students.

Think about ...

Use your 'sociological imagination' to identify possible explanations for poverty in society.

References

MILLS, C. W. (1959) *The Sociological Imagination*. New York: Oxford University Press.

OFFICE FOR NATIONAL STATISTICS (2011) Marriages 2009. [Online] Available from: http://www.ons.gov.uk/ons/rel/vsob1/marriages-in-england-and-wales--provisional-/2009/marriages-summary.html. [Accessed: 12th March 2013].

Status

Status is the position held by an individual or group within society. Status is a form of social stratification and refers to the level of honour and prestige bestowed by others in society. Max Weber defined status as the 'effective claim to social esteem' (1922). Status groups compete with each other to maintain their privileges. It is difficult to objectively measure the degree of status an individual holds and it changes across cultures and throughout time.

How does status differ from class?

There is no agreed definition of social class, but unlike status, it tends to be used to refer to socioeconomic position, often based on occupation. It is possible for an individual to have a high status position, but belong to a lower social class; for example, a Neighbourhood Watch leader may be held in high esteem in their community, but earn the minimum wage as a shop assistant.

In Sociology, a distinction is often made between ascribed status and achieved status.

Ascribed status

An ascribed status is a fixed identity. It is given to an individual, often at birth, and very little can be done to change it. It tends to be inherited from the family and is not shaped by individual effort. Examples include:

➤ Prince Harry has inherited his position as third in line to the throne. This is his birthright.

➤ Paris Hilton has gained fame and fortune as the great-granddaughter of the founder of Hilton Hotels.

Achieved status

An achieved status is gained through effort and merit or talent. It has to be earned. To achieve status an individual may have to undergo training, gain qualifications and compete with others. Examples include:

➤ Alan Sugar is a British billionaire who achieved his status from his electronics company. He was raised in a council flat in the East End of London and became a Lord in 2009.

➤ Jessica Ennis is an athlete who won the heptathlon gold medal in the 2012 Olympic Games. She has been awarded an MBE for her services to athletics.

Unlike ascribed status, achieved status changes over time; for example, an individual may experience a loss in status if they are made redundant.

Think about ...

It is sometimes difficult to define an individual's status. Do you consider the following individuals to have ascribed or achieved status?

a) Samreen studies Law at a prestigious university. Her father is a lawyer and paid for Samreen to attend a private school and for a private tutor. Samreen is working very hard to earn her degree.

b) Michael is a basketball player. He holds the record for the most points scored in a game. At seven foot, he is the tallest player in his league.

Reference

WEBER, M. (1978) *The Economy and Society*. California: University of California Press.

Subculture

A subculture is a group identity related to the dominant culture of society, but with distinct norms and values of its own. Dick Hebdige stated that subcultures bind together like-minded individuals who feel marginalised by mainstream society and allow them to develop their own sense of identity. (Hebdige,1979)

The influence of subculture

Once a subculture enters the public consciousness, it shapes the dominant culture and the line between subculture and dominant culture becomes blurred; for example, in the 1970s punks were anti-establishment and wore clothing for its shock value, such as ripped jeans held together by safety pins. Some years later, mainstream fashion stores sold clothing featuring safety pins. Ironically, something which was anti-materialism had become a commercial success. Hebdige notes that when the dominant society recognises the subculture, its power as a form of resistance begins to die. (Hebdige, 1979)

Key features of subcultures

Paul Hodkinson identified key features from his study of Goths:

1. **A distinctive style:** Although different from the mainstream and despite some diversity within the subculture, Goths are relatively easy to recognise as belonging to the group.

2. **Commitment:** Members are committed to the group to the extent that it influences their lifestyle and everyday life; for example, the clothes they wear and music they listen to.

3. **A strong sense of group identity:** Members must feel part of the group and see themselves as different from outsiders.

Subcultures and signifiers

Hebdige discussed semiotics (the study of signs and symbols) to understand the meanings of youth subcultures. He noted that subcultures took everyday objects and transformed their meanings. The safety pins worn by punks became signifiers which expressed resistance to the mainstream and a marker of identity. (Hebdige, 1979)

A subculture is a difficult term to define; the desire to avoid being labelled means that characteristics of subcultures can be difficult to pin down without using stereotypes and seeming unauthentic. However, there were many noticeable subcultures in the twentieth century.

Examples of 20th-century subcultures

Flappers (1920s)

These were independent young women who valued freedom and rejected Victorian ideas about what was considered to be acceptable behaviour for women. Flappers were notable for:

- dancing in jazz clubs

- casual attitudes towards sex

- smoking cigarettes and drinking alcohol

- wearing shorter hemlines and looser clothing, and rejecting the use of corsets. (Zeitz, 2006)

Punks (1970s)

These were young people who were anti-establishment. Punks were associated with:

- anarchy (meaning without rule) and being against the monarchy

- nihilism (belief that life is meaningless)

- the voice for disaffected youth (at a time of mass youth unemployment)

- detaching symbols from their original meanings, e.g. some punks wore swastikas, not as a symbol of racism but to signify a lack of meaning. (Hebdige, 1979)

Hip-hop (1980s)

This subculture originated from Black Americans in New York and has been popular in the UK since the 1980s. It is associated with:

- rap music as a response to urban poverty and racism
- the music of Run-D.M.C., Sugarhill Gang, The Notorious B.I.G., Tupac and, more recently, Eminem and Jay-Z
- East Coast-West Coast rivalry (centred around the rivalry between The Notorious B.I.G. and Tupac, both of whom were murdered)
- MCing, beatboxing, graffiti and break-dancing
- 'bling' and the fostering of materialistic values, a criticism of hip-hop artists who have had commercial success and were believed to have 'sold out'.

Are subcultures still relevant?

There were many more subcultures present in the twentieth century than shown here, and some people still consider these subcultures to be a part of their identity. For others, a subculture is a rite of passage which they grow out of. In a postmodern society, the idea of subcultures may seem outdated; culture changes quickly and young people choose their identities from a wide range of cultural influences. However, there are still subcultures in Britain, including the following.

Examples of 21st-century subcultures

Hipsters

These are bohemian, urban, middle-class young people, characterised by:

- a dislike of mainstream music, films and fashion labels
- shopping in independent shops for retro and vintage clothing
- consuming the products of a counter-culture without necessarily taking the political messages on board; for example, wearing a Che Guevara T-shirt because it's 'cool' without knowing anything about the Cuban Revolution. (Greif et al, 2010)

> **Freegans**
>
> This is a subculture of anti-consumerists who eat food discarded by shops. The word freegan comes from 'free' and 'vegan'. Freegans are associated with:
>
> - reducing waste – approximately a third of the food bought in the UK is thrown away (WRAP, 2008)
> - 'urban foraging' – searching through supermarket bins for food still in its packaging which can be eaten
> - wild foraging – living off the land
> - free markets where goods can be swapped. (Freegan.info, 2012)

Think about ...

With reference to the third feature of subcultures identified by Hodkinson, explain why 'chavs' would not necessarily be considered a subculture.

See also:
Deviance; Moral panic.

References

ALDERMAN, N. (2010) Steampunk Culture: An Introduction. *The Guardian*. 8th August. [Online] Available from: http://www.guardian.co.uk/books/2010/aug/08/steampunk-lincoln. [Accessed: 2nd January 2013].

FREEGAN.INFO (2012) What is a Freegan? [Online] Available from: http://freegan.info/. [Accessed: 2nd January 2013].

GREIF, M. et al (2010) *What was the Hipster? A Sociological Investigation*. New York: N+1 Foundation.

HEBDIGE, D. (1979) *Subculture: The Meaning of Style*. London: Routledge.

HODKINSON, P. (2002) *Goth: Identity, Style and Subculture*. Oxford: Berg Publishers.

VENTOUR, L. (2008) WRAP Food Waste Report. [Online] Available from: http://wrap.s3.amazonaws.com/the-food-we-waste-executive-summary.pdf. [Accessed: 2nd January 2013].

ZEITZ, J. (2006) *Flapper: A Madcap Story of Sex, Style, Celebrity and the Women Who Made America Modern*. New York: Three Rivers Press.

Symbolic interactionism

Symbolic interactionism is a micro theory which addresses interpersonal action – how people communicate with each other and the shared meanings of symbols that help individuals to understand society; for example, a handshake is a symbol for a greeting and a mark of respect. Symbolic interactionism became prominent in the 1920s and 1930s. Its key proponents are George Hubert Mead, Charles Horton Cooley, Erving Goffman and Herbert Blumer.

What is a symbol?

A symbol is something which represents something else; for example, a Rolex watch could be a symbol of wealth, a school prefect badge is a symbol of responsibility (or popularity), and language, according to Mead, is a set of symbols.

Think about the word 'chocolate'. We use the word, or symbol, to bring an image of chocolate to mind. You don't need an illustration to picture it. The word might also make you feel happy. All of this is just from seeing the word in print because we have been socialised to think 'symbolically'.

A sense of self

Mead argued that a sense of self develops because we are able to see ourselves as others see us. Blumer stated that this is what separates humans from other animals; we can empathise with each other and think about the meaning of our actions and those of others around us. Human beings are generally very self-conscious about their presentation of self. Consider how often you worry about how something will look to others, or how often a friend says that another friend thinks something about her. You might be told not to worry what others think, but this is difficult as it is a normal part of human interaction.

Dramaturgical analysis

Goffman uses the term 'dramaturgical analysis' to explain how the theatre can be used as a metaphor for life in which individuals are actors. Goffman describes the individual or actor's life as a performance which is carefully stage-managed to maintain the desired presentation of self. Goffman distinguishes between 'front stage' and 'back stage' behaviour. 'Front stage' behaviour is visible to the audience and is the impression the actor wants to get across about themselves. 'Back stage' behaviour is hidden from the audience for the sake of successful impression management. Here the façade drops. For example, a couple hosting a dinner party might be very courteous hosts, but the kitchen might be a mess and they might swear at each other out of earshot of the guests because the food is burned.

Today, Facebook can be seen as an example of 'front stage' behaviour as the user tends to reveal what they feel will present them in a positive light; for example, carefully selecting photos in their best outfits with their hair done before a night out, but in reality the user is sitting with their laptop in pyjamas and wearing no make-up.

The 'looking-glass self'

Cooley agrees with Mead that a person's sense of self arises from their interactions with others. He argued that there is no sense of 'I' without the co-relative sense of 'you'. Cooley explains this with reference to a looking-glass: 'each to each a looking-glass, reflects the other that doth pass'. (Cooley, 1902)

The looking-glass self has three stages:

1. We imagine how we appear to another person.

2. We imagine that person's judgement of our appearance.

3. We develop a feeling about that perceived judgement, such as embarrassment or pride.

Evaluation of symbolic interactionism

Strengths	Weaknesses
• It acknowledges that people are not puppets on strings but instead have free will. Symbolic interactionists recognise the creative aspects of human behaviour. • It emphasises the idea that shared meaning is what holds society together. • It emphasises the importance of empathy in understanding society.	• The significance of the structure of the wider society is neglected (this criticism would be made by macro theorists such as functionalists); symbolic interactionism fails to connect the individual's behaviour to its structural setting. • The focus on small-scale interactions means that the claims of symbolic interactionists are difficult to prove and lack generalisability. • It has been criticised for being too subjective and lacking scientific rigour.

Think about ...

According to Mead, people are shaped by the environment they live in, but they also play an active role in shaping that environment. How does this view differ from the macro perspective of Sociology?

See also:
Disneyization;
Self-fulfilling
prophecy;
Weberianism.

References

BLUMER, H. (1969) *Symbolic Interactionism: Perspectives and Methods*. New Jersey: Prentice Hall.

COOLEY, C. H. (1902) *Human Nature and the Social Order*. New York: Charles Scribner's Sons.

GOFFMAN, E. (1971) *The Presentation of Self in Everyday Life*. Harmondsworth: Penguin Books.

MEAD, G. H. (1967) *Mind, Self and Society*. Chicago: Chicago University Press.

Triangulation

Triangulation refers to the use of a mixture of research methods to check the overall validity of the data. The data collected from each method can then help the researcher corroborate their findings; for example, there might be a significant difference in how a research participant behaves during observation and what they say in interviews, so the researcher would probably question the validity of the data collected.

Types of triangulation

It is a common mistake to assume that triangulation is the use of three or more methods (probably because of three points on a triangle); however, it is generally accepted that triangulation means using more than one method. Norman Denzin (1970) identified four types of triangulation:

1. **Data triangulation** uses several sampling techniques to gather data.

2. **Investigator triangulation** employs more than one researcher, or a team of researchers, to interpret the data. This helps to overcome the subjectivities, or opinions, of one researcher.

3. **Theory triangulation** uses different theoretical positions in the interpretation of data; for example, using both a positivist and an interpretivist approach.

4. **Methodological triangulation** uses more than one method for data collection (for example interviews and observation). This is the most common form of triangulation.

The making of a Moonie

Often triangulation involves the combining of quantitative and qualitative methods. An example is Eileen Barker's research. In the 1970s, she researched the lives of members of the Unification Church, a controversial religious movement known as the 'Moonies' which was named after their now deceased leader, Sun Myung Moon, whose followers believed he was the second coming of Christ.

Barker used three research methods:

1. **Questionnaires:** Barker used these to find out *why* people joined the church and to identify trends; for example, whether Moonies were more likely to be former Catholics or Protestants. This method gave Barker quantitative data.

2. **Interviews:** Barker obtained qualitative data from very in-depth and informal interviews (most took several hours) designed to get to know the Moonies better as individuals. This method helped Barker to adapt her questionnaire, making the questions more relevant to the participants.

3. **Participant observation:** Barker was able to build a good relationship with the participants by studying courses on the Unification Church, singing and socialising with the members and attending their rallies. The rapport gained with the members meant they were more likely to trust her and give valid information, and in this way she gained more qualitative data.

Methodological pluralism

Methodological pluralism has a similar meaning to triangulation. It is about using more than one method to get a better overall picture of the group being studied. No research methods are perfect, so using a mixed-methods approach counteracts the limitations of each individual method.

Examples of methodological pluralism from studies:

Anoop Nayak (2006) Displaced Masculinities: Chavs, Youth and Class in the Post-industrial City

Nayak used semi-structured interviews and participant observation to study the masculine identities of young men in Newcastle. He identified two groups: the 'Real Geordies' (family background in skilled labour) and the 'Charver kids' (from communities with high levels of unemployment). The interviews took place in school and were used to find out about the participants' values and interests. The observations took place on nights out at weekends. The fact that Nayak lived on a run-down estate meant that he could, in some ways, empathise  with the 'Charver kids' which helped him to gain a rapport. The use of methodological pluralism gave Nayak increased access to the group. He could not rely on the interviews alone with the 'Charver kids' as their school attendance was very poor.

Despite the benefits of using more than one method, researchers may stick to one, as it is usually cheaper and quicker. A mixed-methods approach can be time-consuming when interpreting data if the researcher gets contradictory results from the different methods.

Think about ...

Identify a study that you have learned about on your Sociology course that used more than one research method. What did the researchers gain from this approach?

See also:
Interpretivism;
Positivism;
Reliability;
Validity.

References

BARKER, E. (1984) *The Making of a Moonie: Choice or Brainwashing?* Oxford: Basil Blackwell.

DENZIN, N. K. (1970) *The Research Act in Sociology*. Chicago: Aldine.

NAYAK, A. (2006) Displaced Masculinities: Chavs, Youth and Class in the Post-industrial City. *Sociology*. 40.

Underclass

The term 'underclass' appears in the heading below in inverted commas because it is a controversial concept; its very existence is hotly disputed. Walter Garrison Runciman defined 'underclass' as a group of people beneath the working classes 'whose roles place them more or less permanently at the economic level where benefits are paid by the state to those unable to participate in the labour market at all'. (Runciman, 1990)

Definitions of an 'underclass'

There are many different definitions of an 'underclass'. For the American author Charles Murray, the definition includes more than long-term dependency on benefits. He argues that the underclass is a type of poverty based on 'undesirable behaviour' (Murray, 1990) including the following characteristics:

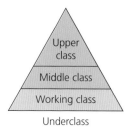

➤ crime

➤ illegitimacy (an outdated term for children born to unmarried parents)

➤ failure to hold down a job.

What causes an underclass?

In 1989, Murray visited Britain, describing himself as a visitor from a plague area who had come to see whether the disease was spreading (Green, 1994 , cited in Murray, 1996). He predicted that the problem of Britain's underclass would worsen. In 1994, he came back to Britain and found that the numbers of violent crimes and births outside of marriage had increased.

For Murray, the underclass reproduces itself in a vicious cycle as follows:

➤ A young woman from a 'broken' home gets pregnant by a young man who is unemployed, takes drugs and commits violent crime.

➤ The young woman is abandoned by the father of her baby and she relies on state benefits.

➤ Without a male role model, the mother struggles to socialise her son to become a responsible young man. He repeats the behaviour of his father.

➤ Her son gets a girl pregnant and leaves her like his father left his mother.

The Welfare State and New Right politics

Murray's views of a British underclass are associated with New Right politics of the time. The then Prime Minister, Margaret Thatcher, stated that there was 'no such thing as society' and she advocated a 'rolling back' of the Welfare State. She wanted families to look after themselves. In addition, Thatcher's successor, John Major, launched a 'Back to Basics' campaign in 1993 in which he aimed to restore traditional family values. However, this campaign was seen as unrealistic (in this year the divorce rate was at an all-time high). The campaign was also seen as hypocritical as there were news stories at the time about the adultery of cabinet members.

Evaluation

While Murray won the support of many conservatives, his views were heavily criticised. Key criticisms include:

➤ **Value judgements:** Murray's theory has been criticised for making moral judgements about how people live. The language indicates his value judgements; for example, he described single mothers as a 'breeding ground' for the underclass.

➤ **Attack on single mothers:** Many single mothers provide good role models. They seem to be blamed in Murray's theory for educational underachievement. However, this is often due to poverty, not the mother herself.

➤ **Work shy:** Murray claims that the underclasses are unwilling to take work available to them. While some members of society are unwilling to work, for many finding a job is difficult. Totaljobs reported that in 2012 there were on average 17 applicants per job advertised. (Watson, 2012)

➤ **'Overgenerous' benefit system:** The term benefit 'scrounger' rather than benefit claimant is commonly heard today. However, since April 2013 there has been a cap on benefits including Jobseeker's Allowance and Income Support. (Wilson, 2012)

Think about ...

Explain how television talk shows like *Jeremy Kyle* may further the demonisation of a so-called 'underclass'.

See also:
Poverty.

References

JOYCE, R. (2012) *Thoughts on a benefit cap*. Institute for Fiscal Studies. [Online] Available from: http://www.ifs.org.uk/publications/6012. [Accessed: 13th January 2013].

MURRAY, C. (1996) *Underclass: The Crisis Deepens*. London: The IEA in association with *The Sunday Times*.

RUNCIMAN, W. G. (1990) How many classes are there in contemporary British Society? *Sociology*. 24 (3).

THATCHER, M. (1987) Interview for *Woman's Own* ('No Such Thing as Society'). In *Margaret Thatcher Foundation: Speeches, Interviews and Other Statements*. London.

WATSON, T. (2012) Totaljobs Barometer Report: Q2 2012. [Online] Available from: http://blog.totaljobs.com/barometer-report-q2-2012. [Accessed: 13th January 2012].

WILSON, W. (2012) The Household Benefit Cap. [Online] Available from: http://www.parliament.uk/briefing-papers/sn06294. [Accessed: 13th January 2013].

Validity

Validity refers to whether or not the data collected during research gives a true and accurate picture of the concept which is being investigated.

Data can be valid without necessarily being reliable.

How to gain valid data

Valid data is an 'accurate reflection of social reality' (Haralambos & Holborn, 2000), therefore data can be valid without being **reliable** at the same time. For example, using statistics to measure school exclusion and truancy rates will be reliable and will show the key trends; however, the statistics won't give the researcher any clues about the reasons for truancy or the impact of this behaviour on the students. Therefore, to gain valid data on this subject, a sociologist may choose to do some unstructured interviews or participant observations.

Statistics alone lack the depth needed to describe the motivations and meanings attached to behaviours. As a result, many **interpretivist** sociologists use qualitative research methods in order to collect valid data. (Haralambos & Holborn, 2000)

Validity and questionnaires

Questionnaires and surveys produce reliable and quantitative data, but the validity of the data can be debated for the following reasons:

➤ The researcher lacks any relationship with the respondent and, as a result, they glean a fairly detached picture of their views.

➤ The respondent might lie when completing a survey or be guilty of 'right answerism'; in other words, they give the response they believe the researcher wants to hear, or that is most appropriate and in line with social norms, rather than their true feelings.

➤ A questionnaire often includes several closed questions for ease of data analysis, yet a respondent's actual answer may not quite fit into the given categories, such as 'always', 'sometimes', 'never'.

Validity and participant observation

In the 1960s, 'James Patrick' (a pseudonym) conducted a covert participant observation of a gang in Glasgow. One member of the gang, 'Tim', knew who he was, but the other members did not. By doing this sort of research, Patrick was able to gain valid, qualitative data which allowed him to get a true picture of gang culture.

In order to research subject matter of this nature, a method such as a questionnaire, formal interview or using statistics would not produce a realistic picture; it would also be impossible to carry out. So, despite the ethical issues raised by Patrick's study, he was able to gain the valid data needed to truly understand Glasgow gang behaviour.

Think about ...

Consider the ways in which anonymity can improve validity. Are there any problems with anonymity? (Anonymity means that the respondent's identity is not revealed.)

See also: Ethics in research; Interpretivism; Qualitative data; Quantitative data; Reliability.

References

HARALAMBOS, M. & HOLBORN, M. (2000) *Sociology: Themes and Perspectives*. 5th Ed. London: HarperCollins Publishers.

PATRICK, J. (1973) *A Glasgow Gang Observed*. London: Methuen.

Values

Values are general principles about human behaviour in society. They are beliefs about what is seen as important in life. Whereas norms are specific rules, values are the beliefs behind the norms and the reasons for the norms' existence; for example, the value behind the norm of revising for an exam is achievement. Many values are taught during primary socialisation, but others are learned later in life.

Core values

Many businesses state their core values on their websites as a means of attracting potential customers and employees. These often include: efficiency, integrity, respect for employees, equal opportunities and, increasingly, environmental responsibility. Public schools often express their values through a school song and most schools and universities have a motto, often in Latin. Examples include:

➤ University of Nottingham: *Sapientia urbs conditur* (A city is founded on wisdom)

➤ University of Manchester: *Cognitio, sapientia, humanitas* (Knowledge, wisdom, humanity).

Values and culture

Values vary across time and culture. In many Western societies, wealth and consumerism are core values. Members of society are encouraged to work hard for material rewards such as designer clothing, cars and the latest technology. A lot of people pay for goods with credit cards and loans, whereas in the past there was an expectation to live within one's means. A lottery win is portrayed as the ultimate level of happiness by the media.

For Buddhists, however, happiness is about letting go of an attachment to material possessions; they believe the constant striving for more causes misery.

Functionalism and values

Functionalists state that it is very important to reach a consensus (agreement) on shared values to ensure that society runs smoothly. The functionalist Emile Durkheim believed that members of society are bound together in a social solidarity. Having shared values prevents conflict in society as people want the same things.

Marxism and values

Marxists disagree with the functionalist view. They claim that far from being agreed, many values are imposed by the bourgeoisie and that conflict is eventually inevitable if members of society are being oppressed by a ruling-class ideology.

It could be argued that as society is now far more culturally diverse than when most functionalists were writing, the UK is now characterised by a wide diversity of values. However, people may belong to different cultures but share some core values (what is seen as truly important in life). Core values in the UK may include:

Forgiveness	Tolerance	Loyalty	Success
Freedom	Respect	Love	Beauty
Compassion	Confidence	Discipline	Contentment

Think about ...

Look at the values in the table. Which four do you think are most important for society? How did you reach your decision?

See also:
Culture; Norms; Socialisation.

Verstehen

The German concept 'Verstehen' means 'understanding'. It is used in Sociology to describe empathy in research. (Empathy is being able to understand the feelings of others due to shared experiences.) It involves the researcher seeing the social world as the participant sees it. Gaining Verstehen means no longer seeing a culture through the eyes of a detached outsider; instead the researcher becomes part of the group.

Weber and interpretivism

Max Weber argued that to truly understand meaning, researchers must experience the culture for themselves. Verstehen was a central concept in his work. He argued that it is very important to understand the meaning individuals attach to their actions. He said of the social sciences: 'We can accomplish something which is never attainable in the natural sciences, namely the subjective understanding of the action of the component individuals.' (Weber, 1968)

Examples of Verstehen in research

To gain Verstehen, an ethnographic approach to research is required. Ethnography is the study of a culture. Participant observation is the main method used in ethnographic studies. Here are some examples.

Polly Toynbee: Hard Work: Life in Low-pay Britain

In 2002 Polly Toynbee, a journalist for *The Guardian*, was challenged by the charity Work Action on Poverty to live on £4.10 per hour (the national minimum wage at the time) for the 40 days of Lent. Toynbee rented a flat on a council estate in one of the poorest areas of London. She didn't seek out the very worst jobs as she wanted to show what life was like for many ordinary working people in Britain, not at the extremes. She worked in low-paid jobs, including telesales, early morning cleaning and as a hospital porter. Toynbee gained Verstehen with working people living in poverty by losing the luxuries of her lifestyle as a journalist; instead, she had to catch buses at 4 a.m., keep to a very strict budget and live in a block of flats frequented by drug addicts.

Sudhir Venkatesh: Gang Leader for a Day

Venkatesh set out to research the lives of the urban poor in Chicago when he was a first-year graduate student. He tried to get people in a housing project to complete a survey about poverty. Here he met the gang leader of the Black Kings, JT. Venkatesh befriended JT, and over the next seven years he got to know the  neighbourhood crack dealers and observed their culture first hand. He gained Verstehen by being allowed by JT to become gang leader for a day, making all decisions on behalf of the gang. He was able to explode some myths during his research. Venkatesh found that dealing crack was not very profitable for people at the street level and that they looked after the older people in their community.

Advantages of Verstehen

➤ Gaining first-hand experience is an excellent way of understanding the culture of others because of the potential for high validity. Taking part in a group's activities uncovers insights that cannot be gained from a survey.

➤ An empathetic approach means that the researcher can gain a good rapport or relationship with the participants. When a rapport is established, participants are more likely to trust the researcher and therefore be more comfortable to reveal their true feelings.

Disadvantages of Verstehen

➤ There is a danger of 'going native'; seeing things through the eyes of participants can result in a lack of objectivity.

➤ Positivists would criticise this approach, claiming that it lacks objectivity and scientific rigour.

Think about ...

Identify an example of a sociological researcher you have learned about who gained Verstehen with their sample. What were the strengths and weaknesses of this approach to research?

See also:
Interpretivism;
Validity;
Weberianism.

References

TOYNBEE, P. (2003) *Hard Work: Life in Low-pay Britain*. London: Bloomsbury Publishing.

VENKATESH, S. (2008) *Gang Leader for a Day: A Rogue Sociologist Takes to the Streets*. New York: Penguin.

WEBER, M., ROTH, G. (ed.) & WITTICH, C. (ed.) (1978) *Economy and Society: An Outline of Interpretive Sociology*. California: University of California Press.

Warm bath theory

The 'warm bath theory' is a metaphor that was used by the functionalist Talcott Parsons to describe the role of the family. Parsons argued that the family eased the stresses of everyday life just like a warm bath. For example, a man returns home from a difficult day; his wife offers sympathy which then relieves his stress, making the thought of returning to work the following day more bearable.

The functionalist role of the family

The warm bath theory relates to what Parsons sees as a key function of the family – the stabilisation of adult personalities. Parsons stated that within marriage, husbands and wives give one another emotional support. In addition, parents can get away from the stresses of the adult world by playing with their children and feeling like children themselves again. The family therefore supports the wider society by relieving stress which, if it were left in the workplace, would cause disharmony and conflict.

The Marxist role of the family

The 'warm bath theory' is similar to the Marxist concept of the 'safety valve'. The neo-Marxist Eli Zaretsky argued that the family works as a safety valve whereby proletarian men who feel powerless and frustrated with their working lives return home and take out their frustrations on their wives instead of on their bosses or the bourgeoisie, which could result in them being sacked. So whereas for Parsons the warm bath theory is viewed as a positive function of the family, for Zaretsky the safety valve is a way for the bourgeoisie to exploit families for their own gains.

Criticism of the warm bath theory

➤ Feminists claim that the warm bath theory is sexist as it seems to benefit men at the expense of women. It is the woman who is providing the warm bath environment for her husband by taking on his stresses. What about the stresses of the woman?

➤ Parsons' views of the family are perhaps too harmonious. The warm bath theory provides a happy families image that ignores the 'dark side' of family life. For some, the family is a dangerous place where domestic violence occurs. On average two women a week are killed by their partner or ex-partner. (Refuge, 2012)

➤ The warm bath theory is a dated concept. It was more applicable in the 1950s when Parsons was writing because then many women were housewives. Today the majority of women work in paid employment.

Think about ...

If the warm bath theory is seen as a dated concept, how would you describe the role of the family in today's society? Can you identify a more appropriate metaphor?

See also:
Conjugal roles.

References

PARSONS, T. & BALES, R. F. (1955) *Family, Socialisation and Interaction Process*. New York: Free Press.

REFUGE (2012) Every week, another two women escape domestic violence. [Online] Available from: http://refuge.org.uk/about-us/campaigns/early-warning-signs/. [Accessed: 3rd January 2013].

ZARETSKY, E. (1976) *Capitalism, the Family and Personal Life*. New York: Harper and Row.

Weberianism

Weberianism is a theory based on the work of Max Weber (born 1864). He is widely regarded as one of the founding fathers of Sociology along with Karl Marx and Emile Durkheim. Weber was a key proponent of social action theory; he argued against the positivist scientific approach to Sociology and claimed instead that interpreting the meanings of individuals' actions in society was more important.

Weber's debate with Marx

Writing some 60 years after Marx, Weber was both influenced by and critical of his work. Weber disagreed with Marx on two key points:

1. **Focus on the economy:** Marx believed that all areas of society were shaped by the economy. Politics, religion and the law were not important in their own right, but instead they formed part of the superstructure and were ideological apparatus of state control; they were institutions which supported the economy for capitalist gain. For Weber, the economy was important, but so too were religion, the law and politics; these different aspects of society overlapped and no one area dominated.

2. **Criticism of society:** For Marx, the purpose of Sociology was to encourage social change. He was critical of inequality in society and saw it as the goal of Sociology to address such inequality. Weber was more interested in finding meaning in society rather than criticising it. He tried to approach Sociology in a politically neutral manner.

Key Weberian concepts

Social action
These are the actions orientated towards other people. Weber believed that, to understand the motives behind an

individual's action, researchers need to put themselves in the position of the individual.

Class

Unlike Marx, Weber believed that the economy was not the only determining factor of social class; instead, he saw class as being based on an individual's market situation and life chances. By this, Weber meant that an individual's ability to access goods and services depends not only on the possession of property but also on their income, work-based skills and academic qualifications. For example, a head teacher does not own the school, but is nevertheless in a higher class position because of their bargaining power; a head teacher has the ability to command high pay due to education and experience.

Status

Weber defined a status group as a group of people who share the same level of social prestige or honour in society. They will have similar lifestyles and shared status symbols to represent their identities. Ken Morrison explained that while class is based on market situation, status is based on consumption or what the individual spends their money on. (Morrison, 2000)

Party

Weber used this term to refer to political power. Political parties have to compete with each other for power in the form of votes. While political power might denote status and can be used or exploited for financial gain, Weber sees class, status and power as somewhat separate. Social class position does not necessarily go hand in hand with political power; for example, a trade union leader from a working-class background arguably holds greater political power than a middle-class professional who does not vote.

Weber's views on authority in society

Weber is also known for the distinctions he made between three types of authority or leadership in society:

1 Charismatic authority

This is the authority of leaders who influence the behaviour of others and inspire them to follow them because of their reputation and strong character. They are persuasive individuals who have loyal followers because they are seen as special and they often promise change. Examples include Mahatma Gandhi, Martin Luther King and Adolf Hitler. (It may be surprising to see Hitler included in this list, but charismatic leaders do not necessarily have a positive influence on society. Through Nazi propaganda, Hitler made a strong connection with thousands of voters for society.)

2 Traditional authority

This is the authority of individuals who are able to exercise power based on their ascribed status or birthright. Examples include the royal family; the Queen has the right to rule because she was born to do so.

3 Rational–legal authority

This is the authority that stems from bureaucracy or the administration of rules and laws. For example, a teacher might be obeyed because of the existence of school rules rather than their personality; the police might be obeyed because they have the weight of the law behind them. Here individuals obey because they have to, rather than through choice, as law, in theory, applies to everyone.

Neo-Weberian concepts

Neo-Weberian thinkers have attempted to apply Weber's theory to more recent times ('neo' means new). Two neo-Weberians are included in this book: Frank Parkin wrote about the Weberian concept of social closure; George Ritzer applied the Weberian concept of bureaucracy to his theory of McDonaldization.

Evaluation of Weberianism

Strengths	Weaknesses
• The fact that Weber acknowledged that class position was based on more than the individual's relationship to the means of production means that he is able to account for the growth of the middle classes. • The theory is not economically deterministic; Weber recognises the importance of other sources of power such as religion and politics. • Weber approached Sociology from a politically neutral position. He did not allow his own political views to shape his work.	• We mostly read how Weber criticised Marx. Marxists today would perhaps criticise Weber for not seeing challenging inequality as the key role of Sociology. • Weber has been criticised for downplaying the importance of the economy. It is unusual in capitalist society to find an individual who has great political power and yet a low class position; for example, the British government's Cabinet ministers in 2013 are predominantly from upper- or middle-class backgrounds. • Lee and Newby (1983, cited in Haralambos & Holborn, 2000) accused Weber of methodological individualism, meaning that he focused too much on the actions of individuals rather than the constraints of the structure of society.

Think about ...

Summarise the differences between Weber's and Marx's approach to Sociology.

See also:
Marxism;
McDonalidization;
Social closure;
Status; Symbolic
interactionism;
Verstehen.

References

HARALAMBOS, M. & HOLBORN, M. (2000) *Sociology: Themes and Perspectives*. 5th Ed. London: HarperCollins Publishers.

HOLTON, R. J. & TURNER, B. S. (1989) *Max Weber on Economy and Society*. London: Routledge.

MORRISON, K. (2000) *Marx, Durkheim, Weber: Formations of Modern Social Thought*. London: Sage Publications.

White-collar crime

The criminologist Edwin Sutherland defined white-collar crime as 'crime committed by a person of respectability and high social status in the course of his occupation' (1949). It can be distinguished from blue-collar crime, the crimes associated with the working class. The stereotypical view of crime is to see it as a working-class problem; the impact of white-collar crime is often overlooked, but arguably it costs society more. It includes corporate and occupational crime.

Corporate crime

This is crime committed by a business against its employees or the general public. Examples include:

➤ Tax evasion – a company might avoid paying tax by misrepresenting its profits in its financial accounts

➤ Misleading the consumer – in 2013, many foods advertised as beef were found to contain horse meat which the consumer was unaware of when buying.

Occupational crime

This is crime committed against a business by the employee. Examples include:

➤ Fiddling expenses – an employee might claim for hotels while away on business when they stayed with a friend

➤ Insider trading – this is when employees use insider knowledge to make money on the stock exchange; for example, they may buy or sell shares when they know that a company is subject to a merger or a takeover bid.

The cost of white-collar crime

Based on data from 2008, the National Fraud Authority found that corporate crime in the form of tax evasion cost the UK public over £15 billion a year while benefit fraud cost over £1 billion. Although corporate crime has a greater financial cost, it does not seem to incite the same level of outrage as other crimes. Here are possible explanations.

➤ **A victimless crime:** Corporate crime is often perceived as victimless because the victim and the perpetrator rarely meet (although the public are the victims).

➤ **Detection:** White-collar crime can be more difficult to detect since it takes place behind the closed doors of the office and few members of the public have the necessary insider knowledge to know they are being misled.

➤ **Scapegoating:** Through campaigns advertised in the mass media, people are encouraged to report their neighbours if they suspect them of benefit fraud. Marxists argue that the mass media act as an apparatus of state control which has a bias in favour of the middle classes, who control it.

➤ **Perceptions of acceptability:** Janice Goldstraw-White researched convicted white-collar criminals. A bank manager convicted of major forgery stated in an interview: 'It's not like I'm a *real* criminal.' Goldstraw-White concluded that many white-collar criminals see themselves as a 'breed apart' from other offenders.

Think about ...

Is the public perception of white-collar crime changing?

See also:
Deviance;
Left and right
realism.

References

GOLDSTRAW-WHITE, J. (2010) It's not like I'm a real criminal. *Sociology Review*. 200 (2).

HYDE, D. (2010) Tax Evasion Costs Treasury 15 Times More Than Benefit Fraud. *Citywire Money.* 22nd January. [Online] Available from: http://citywire.co.uk/money/tax-evasion-costs-treasury-15-times-more-than-benefit-fraud/a378274. [Accessed: 16th March 2013].

SUTHERLAND, E. (1949) *White Collar Crime*. New York: Holt, Rinehart and Winston.

Index